M000286983

Praises for *Leading with Vulnerability*

"Jacob takes a wonderfully thorough look at one of the most important—and lacking—qualities in leaders. And he does so with a raw and honest approach that makes his point all the more powerful(!)"

—Patrick Lencioni,
best-selling author of *The Five Dysfunctions of a Team* and *The Six Types of Working Genius*

"Vulnerability, in today's complex, uncertain world, is simply a fact. Good leaders don't shy away from, but instead acknowledge and embrace this reality. Backed by a study of 100 CEOs and a survey of 14,000 employees, Jacob has put together an invaluable resource to help leaders navigate vulnerability to achieve more, build trust, and drive performance.

—Amy C. Edmondson,
professor, Harvard Business School;
author of *The Right Kind of Wrong:
The Science of Failing Well* (Atria, 2023)
and *The Fearless Organization* (Wiley 2018)

"Given all the blather about authentic and vulnerable leadership, some take it as a signal to abandon accountability and just let the world know how you're feeling. According to Jacob, what you want is the combination of vulnerability PLUS leadership—as in 'I don't know, but here's our plan for how we're going to find out.' This book offers many wonderful examples and insights for how leaders can put the power of vulnerability to work. You'll never think about leadership the same way again."

—Rita McGrath,
author of *Seeing Around Corners*;
professor, Columbia Business School

"This book is a game-changer for current and aspiring leaders. Jacob provides readers with a treasure trove of insights on how to connect with team members, unlock potential, and drive business performance. I wish I had this book when I was entering the business world!"

—Frank Blake,
former chairman &
CEO, The Home Depot

"*Leading with Vulnerability* is a superpower that many leaders struggle with. It creates human connection, trust, and unlocks the potential of those around you. This excellent book teaches leaders how to do just that. Filled with stories and research this is a must-read for any leader!"

—Niren Chaudhary,
chief executive officer,
Panera Bread & Panera Brands

"Vulnerability is a topic that is uncomfortable for so many. Jacob tackles this head on with insights from CEOs to help leaders understand that vulnerability shouldn't just be discussed but also utilized as a superpower to lead through change."

—Jason McGowan,
founder & CEO, Crumbl Cookies

"*Leading with Vulnerability* is a masterclass in balancing the human connection with the competence needed to lead successfully in today's complex world. Jacob has artfully distilled the wisdom of over 100 CEOs and 14,000 employees into a compelling, actionable guide. This book will reshape your understanding of leadership and empower you to create deeper connections and drive greater impact. An essential read for leaders at every level."

—Erin Meyer,
NYT best-selling author of
No Rules Rules and *The Culture Map*

"The leaders of today and tomorrow are discovering vulnerability as a leadership requirement and a tool for advancement in our increasingly transparent world. Jacob's insights are exactly the kind of modern and realistic thinking we need in today's business climate. As organizations adapt to the effects of AI, flexible working, and climate change, it will be the leaders who harness vulnerability rather than avoid it who will drive sustainable growth in their industries. I encourage leaders to learn from the great examples in this book and apply them rigorously."

—Lorenzo Simonelli,
chairman & CEO, Baker Hughes

LEADING

WITH

VULNERABILITY

LEADING
WITH
VULNERABILITY

UNLOCK YOUR **GREATEST SUPERPOWER** TO
TRANSFORM YOURSELF, YOUR TEAM,
AND YOUR ORGANIZATION

JACOB MORGAN
Foreword by Marshall Goldsmith

WILEY

Copyright © 2024 by Jacob Morgan. All rights reserved.

Published by John Wiley & Sons, Inc., Hoboken, New Jersey.
Published simultaneously in Canada.

No part of this publication may be reproduced, stored in a retrieval system, or transmitted
in any form or by any means, electronic, mechanical, photocopying, recording, scanning, or
otherwise, except as permitted under Section 107 or 108 of the 1976 United States Copyright
Act, without either the prior written permission of the Publisher, or authorization through
payment of the appropriate per-copy fee to the Copyright Clearance Center, Inc., 222
Rosewood Drive, Danvers, MA 01923, (978) 750-8400, fax (978) 750-4470, or on the web
at www.copyright.com. Requests to the Publisher for permission should be addressed to the
Permissions Department, John Wiley & Sons, Inc., 111 River Street, Hoboken, NJ 07030, (201)
748-6011, fax (201) 748-6008, or online at http://www.wiley.com/go/permission.

Trademarks: Wiley and the Wiley logo are trademarks or registered trademarks of John Wiley
& Sons, Inc. and/or its affiliates in the United States and other countries and may not be used
without written permission. All other trademarks are the property of their respective owners.
John Wiley & Sons, Inc. is not associated with any product or vendor mentioned in this book.

Limit of Liability/Disclaimer of Warranty: While the publisher and author have used their
best efforts in preparing this book, they make no representations or warranties with respect
to the accuracy or completeness of the contents of this book and specifically disclaim any
implied warranties of merchantability or fitness for a particular purpose. No warranty may be
created or extended by sales representatives or written sales materials. The advice and strategies
contained herein may not be suitable for your situation. You should consult with a professional
where appropriate. Further, readers should be aware that websites listed in this work may have
changed or disappeared between when this work was written and when it is read. Neither the
publisher nor authors shall be liable for any loss of profit or any other commercial damages,
including but not limited to special, incidental, consequential, or other damages.

For general information on our other products and services or for technical support, please
contact our Customer Care Department within the United States at (800) 762-2974, outside
the United States at (317) 572-3993 or fax (317) 572-4002.

Wiley also publishes its books in a variety of electronic formats. Some content that appears in
print may not be available in electronic formats. For more information about Wiley products,
visit our web site at www.wiley.com.

Library of Congress Cataloging-in-Publication Data is Available:

ISBN 9781119895244 (Cloth)
ISBN 9781119895251 (ePub)
ISBN 9781119895268 (ePDF)

Cover Design and Illustration: © Gerard Allen T. Mendoza.
Author Photo: © Nancy Rothstein Photography

SKY10053502_081823

To Noah and Naomi, may you always lead with vulnerability, and I will try to do the same. To my wife, Blake, you are simply amazing and I love you. To my family, thank you for your support and love. And to you, the reader, thank you for picking up this book and going on this important journey.

Contents

Foreword

Dr. Marshall Goldsmith

As an executive coach for over 40 years, my mission has been to help successful leaders get even better for the sake of their companies, teams, and their own lives. Throughout my career, I have observed that one of the most common struggles among smart and talented individuals is their vulnerability. Too often, leaders are hesitant to show vulnerability, fearing that it will be perceived as a sign of weakness. This can lead to a command-and-control approach that is far less effective than one in which leaders cultivate humility, trust, and vulnerability within their teams. Many leaders understand this important point, but they struggle to find ways to live out this shift in behavior on a daily basis.

Leading with Vulnerability offers a practical and proven approach to understanding vulnerability and how to incorporate it into your leadership style. Jacob offers powerful insights and personal revelations on what it means to be a competent, vulnerable leader. He has interviewed top leaders around the world, sharing their experiences and offering readers a grounded look at how to live out vulnerability amid challenging situations. By providing actionable advice and pulling together these stories, Jacob has created a book that empowers readers to harness their vulnerability and become the leaders they were meant to be.

It's essential for leaders to understand that vulnerability is not a license to share everything about yourself, including your fears and insecurities, with your team. Vulnerability should not be a replacement for good leadership, nor should it be an excuse for poor decision-making. In fact, vulnerability should be balanced with good judgment, thoughtful communication, and a clear understanding of what information is appropriate to share with your team. As *Leading with Vulnerability* highlights, being vulnerable doesn't mean being weak but rather being confident enough in yourself and your abilities to be honest about your mistakes, limitations, and uncertainties. It's about cultivating a culture of trust, openness, and honesty that enables your team to thrive and your organization to achieve its goals.

If you are a leader looking to build better relationships, foster constructive work cultures, and realize the full potential of your team and organization, this is the book you need to read. It is a timely and important reminder that true strength comes from embracing vulnerability, rather than hiding behind a façade of control and power. With its focus on personal growth and development, this book is not just for leaders but for anyone looking to build better relationships and create a culture of vulnerability and trust within their team or organization.

■ ■ ■

Dr. Marshall Goldsmith is the *Thinkers50* #1 Executive Coach and *New York Times* bestselling author of *The Earned Life*, *Triggers*, and *What Got You Here Won't Get You There*.

Introduction

Where It All Began

A loud explosion went off. "We have to run now!" Klara said. Another barrage of explosions started and it felt like the world was on fire. Klara grabbed her 4-year-old daughter, Genya, who could barely make sense of what was happening. It was the beginning of World War II. Without having time to grab anything, they ran out into the night along with thousands of other people. As they ran, they saw Zoya, a young girl Genya's age, who was running around screaming; her mother had just hung herself after finding out her husband was killed in battle. Klara grabbed Zoya and all three of them fled.

Klara and the two girls came to an open field. They had to cross the field as low flying fighter pilots dropped bombs on them. There was chaos everywhere, and Klara lost the hand of one of the girls. Faced with the choice of all of them getting killed and saving herself and one little girl, Klara and the other girl continued on to safety. Eventually Klara and the girl got to a train station. The train traveled over a river when another explosion went off and the bridge the train was on was destroyed. The train and all of the passengers plummeted into the cold dark water below.

They crawled over dead bodies until they emerged from the water and walked and hitchhiked their way to Tbilisi, Georgia, where Klara's sister Sonya lived.

Klara Taxer, who only had three years of formal education, found a job as a waitress. They were desperate to find a place to live, and a woman who was renting a 10-foot × 15-foot room in a complex agreed to let them stay with her. Klara and her daughter rented a corner of the room where all they had was a bed. They lived out of their suitcases, which were kept on the floor. The restrooms and kitchens were all communal.

Klara worked double shifts at a restaurant to make a few rubles a month. At night Klara was harassed by the men who frequented the restaurant. Nobody protected her or stood up for her as the men made passes and grabbed her body. Every night after work she would come home and cry. Sometimes Klara would bring home leftovers that other patrons didn't finish so she and her daughter could eat. Genya was alone all day every day until late at night. She had nowhere to go so she would sit in a Catholic church every day because it was safe even though she was Jewish. Genya became friends with the priest, who told her that if she wanted to keep visiting the church she should get baptized, so she did even though she was only five and didn't understand what that meant.

During WWII there was a syphilis scare so the USSR, which Georgia was a part of, mandated that everyone who worked in a restaurant get their blood tested. Klara took her daughter and they went to the home of Alexander Drampov and Nina Egeazarova, an Armenian couple who never had any children. Nina liked Genya so much that she invited her to come over whenever she wanted. Over the years, Alexander and Nina became Genya's unofficial foster parents because Klara worked so much and was never home.

In college, little Genya became fascinated with chess and won a few tournaments. She graduated with a master's degree in history and philology, which is the study of language.

One day in college, a friend of Genya's told her she wanted to set her up with someone who worked at the circus, a Jewish cello player named Alex Begelfor. When Genya first met Alex, she didn't really like him or feel connected to him. But as she and her friend were leaving the circus, a few guys started harassing them.

At that moment, Alex was also walking out with his cello and he defended them, then walked the girls home. A few years later they married and had two kids: Ella and Irena.

In the late 1970s, Klara, Genya, her husband, Alex, and their two daughters had to make a tough choice to flee the Republic of Georgia. Under the communist regime, they didn't feel safe or free. This wasn't easy because Alex loved Georgia. He was known in all of the entertainment circles, had lots of friends, and belonged to a huge community. But, he wanted a better life for his family.

They left Georgia as refugees with no money, no possessions (which were all stolen or confiscated), no legal documents, and without speaking a word of English. The only thing they were able to take out of the country was a few hundred dollars and a half-carat diamond that they snuck out in the handle of a knife. My grandmother still has that diamond in a ring she wears.

From Georgia they went to Italy, which was a transition zone for people leaving Georgia. To make money they sold chachkies at a local flea market, but they barely made enough money to afford eating macaroni and spaghetti for dinner. Genya met a handsome Georgian rugby player while they were both in line at an immigration office. Genya introduced David Mamisashvili to her daughter Ella and eventually they got married.

From Italy they ended up in Australia where Alex and his wife Genya worked as cleaners in a chocolate factory. Eventually Alex became a taxi driver and formed his own string trio, and Genya became a Russian teacher for politicians and officers at a naval academy. Ella and David had two sons: Jacob (me) and my brother, Joshua.

Klara was my great grandmother, Genya is my grandmother, Alex was my grandfather, and Ella and David are my parents. To this day my grandmother doesn't know if she is Genya or Zoya, Klara never told her which girl was lost during the bombings in Ukraine.

When I was young, my parents relocated to the United States; my dad was obsessed with the "American Dream." He changed his last name to "Morgan" to sound more American because nobody was able to pronounce his real last name, Mamisashvili, over company loudspeakers. He moved to the United States first to set up a life before my mom and I joined him from Australia. For several years my mom and dad communicated with each other by sending letters in the mail. He learned to speak English by watching the Johnny Carson and Merv Griffin shows with an English-to-Russian translation dictionary. He would spend hours each day looking in the mirror and trying to mouth out English words properly while he lived in low-income housing in New Jersey. My dad's mom was Sara Bagdadishvili, a stay-at-home mom, and his dad was Yasha Mamisashvili, a store clerk. I never met Sara but I did meet Yasha once when he came to Los Angeles when I was very young. Coming from communism where everything belonged to the government, Yasha couldn't beleive that his son (my dad) was able to create a good life for himself. He thought that my mom and I were actors pretending to be his family and that the house and all of his possessions were owned by the government. My dad showed Yasha an old home video to which he replied "my god, they found me." He believed he was being monitored and followed while in America. Eventually my dad convinved him of the truth. Yasha passed away a few weeks after his visit due to cancer. He just wanted to make sure that his son was happy and was able to make a life for himself.

Although my dad doesn't talk about his past he will, on very rare occasions, share a story with me. Like the time he went from Georgia to Czechoslovakia as a 21-year-old foreign exchange student. A group of students from Georgia traveled with a chaperone who would keep an eye on their every move. My dad loved classic rock and one day while he was exploring Czechoslovakia he picked up a Jimi Hendrix poster. One of the other students on the trip ratted out my dad to get the poster confiscated. To avoid getting in trouble, when my dad was confronted about the poster he said it was actually of Angela Davis, an American member and supporter of the communist party. My dad was lauded for his apparent dedication to communism and was allowed to keep the poster.

My dad just retired from the corporate world after working for decades as an aerospace engineer where he commuted an hour and a half to and from work each day (during COVID he worked from home). My dad sometimes still makes the commute just to play soccer with some of his coworkers. He's 73. My mom is one of the top marriage and family therapists in Los Angeles, and they live 15 minutes away from me.

When you've had to survive like my family, there is no room for weakness. You have to be strong and tough. My mom has always been more open and encouraging of vulnerability and emotion, but ultimately I grew up watching and emulating my dad, who doesn't believe in a trophy for a second place. I remember one time after a soccer tournament my dad and I drove to the coach's house to pick something up. I must have been about 10 years old. We knocked on the coach's door and he handed my dad and me a trophy. My dad looked at the coach and said, "What is this trophy for; they came in last place?" The coach said that they were giving participation trophies so kids wouldn't feel left out. My dad chuckled and said, "That's bullshit. You can keep the trophy," and we got in the car and left. This was an important life lesson for me and it taught me the importance and value of hard work. Life doesn't give participation trophies, and it doesn't care about your problems.

My dad always told me that the world is a jungle and that as a man you always need to be strong and highly competent. Never show weakness under any circumstance, nobody cares about your problems so don't share them, and always be good at what you do, or more specifically, try to be the best at what you do.

I only ever saw my dad cry once, when he was almost killed. As a pedestrian he was struck by a car traveling 45 miles per hour. He lay on the ground covered in blood, screaming. He doesn't remember that, but I do.

My father is a good man—he has a lot of integrity, and as he's gotten older he has become gentle—I see it when he spends time with my kids. He was always there for me, and is a good dad, but the model I had growing up with was a tough guy off the Eastern bloc. Physical and mental fitness were number one. That is what I learned. Don't ever show anyone your emotions, and don't talk much. Even today, when I visit my parent's house, he asks me, "Jacob, how many push-ups can you do?"

That's how I grew up: not being vulnerable and always needing to be strong and not showing weakness. Perhaps you grew up hearing similar messages, especially if you are a male.

As the stress mounted in my family, with two children—one born during COVID—the lack of vulnerability was no longer working for me in my personal life. My wife and I would argue more frequently, it was hard to connect with friends, and my personal and professional relationships didn't feel stable. I didn't quite know how to navigate all of the curve balls life was throwing at me but I wouldn't admit anything was wrong, and I'd never ask for help. I just kept "powering through" life. I also noticed many other people were struggling with vulnerability, especially at work.

Similar to you, I had heard of vulnerability and had an idea of what it was, but was it really that simple? I felt that most of what I was reading and seeing made it sound like if you just share your weaknesses and challenges, then your problems will go away. Perhaps that's a decent solution in your personal life, but what about at work, which has a completely different dynamic? I wondered, can vulnerability really be a powerful way to effectively lead through change?

You're probably a current or aspiring leader who is seeing how the world around you is changing, and you're asking yourself, "How do I lead through this change?" You understand that connecting with people and being able to influence change is one of the most important aspects of leadership, yet you also understand that you need to demonstrate that you are highly capable of doing your job as a contributor to a team and organization. You know what it means to be vulnerable because you have experienced it, but similar to many leaders around the world you're probably wondering if you should be vulnerable at work, why, what the impact is, and how to do it.

You're likely asking the same questions that other leaders are asking:

- What does leading with vulnerability mean and how do I do it?
- What's the impact of leading with vulnerability?
- What happens if I'm vulnerable and it's used against me?
- What are the other attributes that I need to have that help unlock the power of vulnerability?
- How does vulnerability help me lead through change?
- Are there examples, stories, and research about vulnerability and leadership?

I wanted to answer all of these questions and more because if leaders like you can be vulnerable, then others will follow in your footsteps. This will create organizations focused on growth, development, innovation, and, above all, being human. Life is too short to put up a façade of perfection.

I've come to understand the power and value of vulnerability. However, at work vulnerability alone will only get you so far; you need leadership, specifically, competence.

The relationship between vulnerability and competence is an important one to call out. I cannot stress enough that vulnerability cannot be used as a crutch to justify ongoing poor performance, which is something that is unfortunately happening in many organizations. One of the toughest challenges that leaders are faced with is a pervasive mentality of victimhood. The idea that you can substitute for competence and replace it by pointing out all of the reasons for you not having your required level of competency.

Ann Mukherjee is the chairwoman and CEO of Pernod Ricard North America, which has about 1,900 employees. She was born in India and moved to Chicago when she was five years old. When she was 14 years old her mother was killed by a drunk driver and earlier in her life she was the victim of sexual assault by someone who was drunk. You might wonder why someone would want to work for an alcohol company after having such tragic experiences with alcohol. For Ann, it's about using those tragic experiences to make things better for other people. Ann doesn't see herself as a victim but as a powerful change agent who can positively affect the lives of others; she uses her tragedy as fuel for growth and progress.

According to Ann, "As a leader if you're not comfortable with your own chaos and adversity, then you are going to falter. You have to get over your own issues and build resilience as opposed to feeling like a victim, which is one of the dangers facing the workforce today. Turn your pain, fear, and weakness into positive power. Being vulnerable allows you to connect with others to build that resilience but being a vulnerable leader allows you to take that connection and resiliency and do something positive with it to change the world."

Be an owner and take your professional development into your own hands. Don't wait for someone to save you; become your own superhero. Perhaps this is my tough-love immigrant family upbringing speaking, but it's something I have come to believe and something I have observed from the successful CEOs I interviewed, many of whom came from troubled, impoverished, and broken families and who had to rely on their high levels of competence to get to where they are. Competence is crucial, but it's the combination of vulnerability and competence that truly leads to meaningful and significant outcomes.

Vulnerable leaders have both.

I believe that the single most important and impactful thing that you can do for yourself and everyone around you is to lead with vulnerability.

With that, let's begin our vulnerable leader journey together. Are you ready?

I

Who Is a ~~Weak~~ Vulnerable Leader?

1

Panic!

On Thursday, December 23, 2021, a few weeks after signing the contract for this book, I was standing in my bathroom brushing my teeth and I started feeling weird. My body was flooded with adrenaline, my vision became blurry, and my heart started beating out of my chest. My resting heart rate is usually around 57 beats per minute and just standing I was about 130 beats per minute, which is the equivalent of a moderate cardio workout. I thought, "This is it. I'm having a heart attack and I'm going to die," and I was overcome with fear and dread. I felt like a tidal wave of terror just crashed over me.

I screamed for my wife, Blake, who was wrangling our kids for school, and I told her something was wrong with me. I laid down on the bed and then all of a sudden I started shaking uncontrollably. If you've ever seen the Pixar movie *Inside Out* in which emotions are personified by little characters who live in your body, that's what I felt like. As if there were little creatures who were just pushing all sorts of buttons inside of my body and I had no control. It was absolutely terrifying and the most scared I've ever been.

"What the fuck is happening to me?" was all I could think about, followed closely by "Is this the end for me?"

The next few days were really rough because I wasn't able to hear back from my doctor and I had no idea what was happening to me. Was I actually dying? Was it all just in my head? Not knowing was the worst part.

Things calmed down for a few days until it happened again. I asked Blake to drive me to urgent care, which turned me down because they were at capacity with COVID patients; instead, they gave me the address of a hospital with an emergency room. I forced Blake to drive me there and almost checked myself in but Blake talked me out of it.

Finally, the next day I was able to get an appointment with a doctor. They reviewed my lab results and did an EKG and the result was . . . that I'm perfectly healthy and my heart is great!

"Phew," I thought. "Now that I know that, I won't ever have another panic attack again." I just needed a doctor to tell me that I was fine . . . or so I thought. Sure enough, a few days later as I was sitting in my kitchen eating a sandwich, it happened again. "WTF? The doctor told me I was fine, what could possibly be causing this?"

I'm not a vulnerable person and the only human being I know who is less vulnerable than me is my dad. He's the kind of person who could be sick as a dog and if you ask him how he's doing, he'll say "great." When my dad was struck by a car, he spent many weeks in the hospital recovering. I was young when it happened, and one time I went to visit him where he lay in almost a full body cast. I was feeding him ice chips (which gradually melted in his mouth) because he wasn't even able to drink water. He yelled at me and told me he didn't need my help. He doesn't believe in showing weakness of any kind. I have Georgian immigrant parents and the Georgian culture isn't exactly known for being vulnerable or emotional.

I rarely express my emotions or feelings and even have a hard time doing this with family. The phrase "I feel" is very foreign to me but I'm pretty good at saying "I think" or "I know."

As I've come to learn after speaking with therapists and researching panic and anxiety, your body can only handle so much stuffing down of emotions and feelings. Eventually there's no more space left in your body and the physical symptoms begin: a rapid heartbeat, uncontrollable shaking, adrenaline spikes, fear of doom, fever, blurry vision, and the like.

Imagine you have a suitcase you are packing with clothes. Eventually the suitcase fills up but you keep cramming more clothes in there until you realize there is no way it's going to close. So what do you do? You sit on the suitcase and then you force the zipper around it. It shuts for a few minutes and then all of a sudden the seam rips and the suitcase flies open.

Stuffing down emotions and feelings is the same thing. If you try to keep things in, eventually the mind and the body will win. I learned this the hard way.

After diving deeper into what could have caused my panic attacks, it became more clear what a large contributing factor was . . . this book!

The very fact that I had committed to writing a book about vulnerability—something that goes against my very nature—gave me a panic attack. My mind and body just couldn't come to grips with the fact that I was going to have to confront, explore, and dive deep into something I have always stayed away from.

My wife, Blake, told me that by writing this book, I'd be going on a personal and emotional journey to discover more of myself and what it means to be a vulnerable leader, and she was right. I'm on this journey with each and every one of you reading this book.

This is the most important and hardest book I've written, and it's precisely because it explores such a difficult and foreign topic to me—and to many others—vulnerability. During the week or so where I thought I was going to die, I became very vulnerable with friends and family. I cried in my mom's arms, told my friends I was struggling, and had to explain to my kids why I was having a tough time. I saw the deeper connections I was able to make from openly expressing what was happening, the support people gave me, and the candid conversations I was able to have. In one of my team meetings, I shared what I was going through and asked if anyone else had experienced something similar. On my team of 12 people, 4 others had experienced panic attacks. We were able to come together to talk about this and support each other.

I realized how powerful vulnerability could be in both personal and professional environments when done the right way. In my last book, *The Future Leader*, the theme of vulnerability came up quite a bit, and I remembered all of those discussions and conversations I had with CEOs and leaders who shared the importance of connecting with people and creating meaningful relationships, yet also needing to focus on business performance. In that book the skill of Yoda (emotional intelligence including empathy and self-awareness) was the skill that leaders struggled with the most as ranked by employees who reported to them.

I also remembered the specific concerns, issues, and questions that leaders had when it came to vulnerability in the workplace. Thoughts such as being vulnerable without being perceived as weak, how to actually be vulnerable in the right way, why vulnerability alone isn't enough, what happens when vulnerability isn't received well, and many others.

I knew this was a book I had to write because I saw how I struggled with vulnerability and the impact it had on my life and those around me. During my career, I've worked with and interviewed more than 2,000 CEOs and business leaders around the world and I've also seen how much they struggle with vulnerability.

Leading with vulnerability is the single most impactful thing you can do to create connection, drive trust, unlock the potential of those around you, and drive performance if you know the right way to approach it. That's the key, *the right way to approach it*.

This is a book about *you* and how *you* can be a leader who creates trust, connects with your people, unlocks the potential of those around you, and drives business performance.

I embarked on the most in-depth and comprehensive project on vulnerability and leadership that's ever been done. For over two years, I interviewed over 100 CEOs around the world from different industries, including American Airlines, SAP, Hyatt, Northrop Grumman, Dow Chemical, The Home Depot, and dozens of others. Although only 10% of the *Fortune* 500 CEOs are women, I'm proud that more than 25% of the CEOs I interviewed for this book are women. These interviews were done in hour-long discussions and follow-up interviews with a small group of CEOs opting to send in responses via email. I also interviewed the world's leading psychologists and researchers spanning a variety of fields, including emotional intelligence, decision-making, trust, psychological safety, game theory, and organizational behavior.

This book sets itself apart by offering a unique perspective on the power of vulnerability for leaders—a topic not commonly addressed in business education or corporate environments. To gain a deeper understanding, I sought out insights from CEOs, recognizing their paramount responsibility, accountability, and impact in the business world.

Some of the questions I asked these CEOs included (but are not limited to) the following:

- What does being a vulnerable leader/leading with vulnerability mean to you?
- What does vulnerability feel like in your body?
- What makes you feel most vulnerable and why?
- What are other attributes or characteristics that leaders need to have which help unlock the power of vulnerability?
- How can you be vulnerable at work without being perceived as being weak?
- Have you ever been vulnerable at work and had it used against you?
- When you're vulnerable, what is your default defense mechanism?
- What's the impact of being a vulnerable leader?

- Can you be too vulnerable at work?
- How do your personal values influence your willingness to be vulnerable?
- Do you think about the intention or purpose behind being vulnerable?
- What kind of vulnerable leader are you?
- What happens if you work with people who don't believe in being vulnerable?

My discussions with these CEOs were extremely in-depth and personal, so much so that several of them requested to be made anonymous in the book. They shared stories and insights with me that they have never shared before. I am grateful for their openness, transparency, and willingness to be vulnerable with me. I laughed and cried with them. I shared all sorts of emotions and in-the-moment discoveries that I will forever be grateful for.

Last, I teamed up with global leadership firm DDI to survey almost 14,000 employees around the world representing more than 1,500 organizations, 50 countries, and 24 major industry sectors. This was done as a part of their Global Leadership Forecast Series, which is the longest-running global study of leadership aimed at understanding current and future leadership best practices. We also did a follow-up pulse survey with an additional 1,200 participants.

Bringing all of these different perspectives and data points together yielded some truly fascinating insights about leading with vulnerability that I can't wait to share with you.

This book will help you understand what it means to lead with vulnerability; why it's so crucial to your success, your team's success, and your organization's success; and how to actually unlock this amazing superpower for yourself and those around you. Although the strategies and approaches you read about in this book are specifically focused on leadership at work, they can also be applied with positive impact outside of work as well.

The first section of the book introduces what leading with vulnerability means and the crucial difference between vulnerability and vulnerable leadership. You will learn the three truths of vulnerable leaders and how vulnerability saved the lives of some of the toughest men on the planet working on an oil rig. You will discover why you should lead with vulnerability, the importance of being able to identify emotions, why leaders need to have thick skin and not armor, and the three paths people take to becoming vulnerable leaders.

The second section explores why we don't have more vulnerable leaders and what to do about it. You'll hear about the common leadership stereotypes still alive in our organizations today and how to break them, what to learn from working with vulnerable and non-vulnerable leaders, and the importance of using vulnerability early in your career.

In the third section of the book, you'll learn about what makes leaders feel vulnerable and why, including the 10 vulnerability signs and what to do if you spot them. You'll also learn how a bank robber used lemon juice to try to avoid being detected on camera and how that affects our perception of vulnerability, why being a gymnast is more stressful than being a sprinter and why we're all gymnasts, the simple technique you can use when being vulnerable doesn't go as planned, and what we got wrong about the famous Milgram experiment.

The fourth section covers what happens to you physically and emotionally when you are vulnerable and why our perceptions of vulnerability change depending on if we are thinking about ourselves or others. You'll learn the common defense mechanisms we use when feeling vulnerable and how to get past them, the three critical moments leaders face when they are confronted with being vulnerable, and how to respond when someone is vulnerable with you.

The fifth and final section of the book shows you how to lead with vulnerability and unlock your superpower. You'll learn about the five types of vulnerable leader superheroes, the eight attributes of vulnerable leaders, the framework that will help make sure that when you're vulnerable you will see the highest chances of a positive outcome, when being vulnerable is not a good thing, and how to create and climb your vulnerability mountain.

Each section of the book is filled with hard data and stories from the more than 100 CEOs I interviewed to back up and support everything you read.

As a current or aspiring leader, I want you to know that vulnerability is not a weakness; it's a superpower that will transform your life, your team, your company, and the lives of those around you.

Being able to lead through change is one of the toughest challenges facing most organizations around the world, and it's not possible to conquer this challenge without vulnerability. In a rapidly changing environment it's crucial to innovate, work differently, and challenge the status quo. Being able to lead through change is all about people and vulnerability and what creates trust, connection, alignment, growth, and powerful relationships. When these things exist then people will show up with their best ideas for new opportunities and solutions for tackling complex problems, discretionary effort will be unlocked so that customers can be served better, and employees will feel a greater sense of purpose and meaning. Change is hard and uncomfortable, which is why it's so crucial for leaders to bring people together to go through that change as a team and as an organization. These things are all foundational for leading, especially during times of great uncertainty when the path and the outcome are not known.

Leadership is not about hiding behind a mask of invincibility; it's about embracing vulnerability. Unfortunately, most of the leaders around the world don't know that this is a superpower and how to unlock it. When asked if "vulnerability is perceived as a leadership strength, not a weakness [inside of their organizations]" less than 11% of people responded with "definitely true" and

34% said they were "uncertain," which is the equivalent of responding to the question with a response of "definitely false," because if you're uncertain about it, you're likely not going to be vulnerable.

This book will give you the research, the tools, and inspirational and transformational stories from the world's top CEOs so that you can lead with vulnerability.

Billions of people around the world are walking and talking superheroes, and they don't even know it. This is a completely new way to approach being a leader, one that we have all been scared of and didn't feel comfortable talking about. Going forward, this is the only way to lead.

Are you ready to lead with vulnerability?

2

The Vulnerable Leader Equation

On August 20, 1991, Hollis Harris, then CEO of Continental Airlines, told his 42,000 employees to pray for the future of the company. In his memo to employees he said, "We are in a battle here at Continental. We are at war with forces within the company and outside the company."

As Doug Parker, the chairman and former CEO of American Airlines told me, this is being vulnerable, but it's not being a leader. The next day Hollis was fired.

If Hollis was a junior employee who worked in accounting, then those statements would have had minimal impact. Some employees may have taken notice, maybe some would have taken him out to lunch to ask him why he's having a bad day, and he would have received some words of encouragement and support from his leader and life would have moved on. When you're a leader the things you say and do carry more weight and have more impact.

Doug had to go through his fair share of challenges as the CEO of American Airlines including going before Congress and the world to ask for money and support to keep the company from going bankrupt during the pandemic. There were many times he found himself in the parking lot of his company pumping himself up before heading into work and actually trying to suppress his vulnerability. He told me,

As a leader, the last thing the company needs is for anyone to think or believe that American Airlines is in trouble. Especially during the pandemic everyone was reading about how our industry was going down, and the last thing I needed was for my team to think or believe any of that because I didn't believe it. Showing up to work panicked and emotional would not have been the right kind of leadership. I believe vulnerability is a strength but the leadership component has to be there as well because behaving in a way that scares your people is not a good thing for a leader to do.

I heard countless stories like this from CEOs who, during the pandemic, had to stand on the front lines with optimism, courage, vision, and, above all, leadership.

Another such leader is Fleetwood Grobler, the president and CEO of Sasol Limited, a South African energy and chemical company with more than 28,000 employees. He told me the following:

I took over as CEO when the company was in very deep trouble with over $13 billion in debt. I was working in Lake Charles, Louisiana, finishing a project when I was told by the chairman in early October 2019 that the team wanted me to come back and be CEO by the end of October. They asked me to deliver the financial results, which I did for the first time in my life. This was at the end of 2019 and then a few months later in 2020 the pandemic happened. Our company suffered to the point where the banks almost came in and took over because our cash lines and credit flow was up and we were on the hook for $10 billion. In my first town hall, I told the company that I didn't know the answers but I knew we had a great team and that I could get us back on track. I told them that together we would find a way by rebuilding trust with our team and customers.

Great leadership is built on vulnerability and it enables you to unlock your peoples' true ability. It creates trust, builds meaningful professional and personal relationships, unlocks new opportunities, mitigates any threats, and transforms you, your team, and your company for the better.

Whether you lead a company, a department, a team, a community, your family, or yourself, you are a leader. With this title comes the responsibility to lead with vulnerability.

By 2030 we are going to have between 90 million and 440 million leaders around the world. If we take a number in the middle of these two, that's 265 million leaders. These are people who are responsible for the lives of others, for shaping culture and society, creating jobs, speaking up for injustices, and fighting for social causes. True change comes from true leadership; the leaders who embrace vulnerability are the ones who can change the world and guide us to a better future. We cannot create organizational and global change if we don't have the right people to lead us in making that change happen. Jonathan Pertchik is the CEO of TravelCenters of America. With almost 19,000 employees, he has focused on building vulnerability into the culture of the company.

> Failure is built into how our company operates and innovates, which means that vulnerability is built into our culture and this is a conscientious effort. As an example, we may test out five or six different ideas in an area of our business knowing that most are likely to fail but one may give rise to success. We go into this process anticipating failure, mistakes, and challenges. Without vulnerability, there would be no innovation or ability to lead through change because nobody would feel safe to take risks, to think big, or to even talk about their failures. When I came into this role, the company was performing very poorly and the stock was under $9 and today our stock is the highest it's been in 15 years. There is no innovation without leading with vulnerability. It's not easy, it's not comfortable, and it's the only way to lead.

Leadership used to be thought of as this nice cushy job where you got a huge salary, fancy corner office, special parking spot, and more power. Once you became a leader, you made it! You could just coast for the rest of your career and tell other people what to do. The reality is that when you become a leader your job becomes much harder, not easier. Great leaders give a part of themselves to their teams and their company. Simply put, they care more and they do more because that is the role they signed up for (see Figure 2.1).

Figure 2.1   Do more and care more

Frank Blake is the former CEO of The Home Depot; when he left, the company had more than 350,000 employees, and today it has more than 500,000. As CEO, every Sunday he spent half his day writing 200 handwritten cards to his team members.

He would give the card to the team members, take a selfie with them, and tell them he would hang that picture in his office. If they ever came to Atlanta they were invited to see their picture in the CEO's office, which many team members and their families did.

Here's what he told me when we spoke:

As a leader, your people are going to want a piece of you. Every leader is different in how they want to give away a piece of themselves but that's your job, your responsibility, and your privilege. It could be time, a gesture, or a simple act of recognition. When I grew up, I collected baseball cards and the easiest signatures to get were always from the outfielders. Nobody really paid much attention to them and their signatures were easy to get, but when you got their signature you started rooting for them! Leaders need to do the same thing by saying, "I'm giving you a piece of me." Many leaders don't realize that their job is tough and that they are supposed to give more of themselves than anyone else.

Leaders inspire teams, develop a vision and plan, and get people to move in the direction of the vision. Leaders are also responsible for people, organizational resources, creating new products and services, and should be accountable for achieving the goals of the business. They have a unique responsibility and power that means vulnerability cannot be treated, used, or expressed in the same ways it can for everyone else, as you saw in the example of Hollis Harris.

Amy C. Edmondson is a professor of leadership and management at the Harvard Business School and best-selling author of *The Fearless Organization: Creating Psychological Safety in the Workplace for Learning, Innovation, and Growth*. When I interviewed her, she told me the following: "The goal of vulnerability is not to let it all hang out. As a leader of a team or an institution, your primary responsibility is to do what you need to do so that your institution can serve its constituents. Vulnerability can either help when done the right way or it can hurt when approached the wrong way."

Regardless of your culture, background, or race, we all know what vulnerability feels like, and we have all been vulnerable at some point in our lives because we are all human. I acknowledge and respect that there are differences because people are different. This is why it was so important for me to bring in global perspectives across a variety of industries, geographies, and backgrounds. The frameworks, insights, and research are meant to be applicable to anyone. Brené Brown pioneered the topic of vulnerability and her message resonates with millions of people around the world. I've been inspired by her work and aim to build on what she created, specifically focusing on leadership. My hope is that this book will contribute to future discussions and research about this much-needed topic.

I looked at the common themes and patterns that enable leaders to unlock vulnerability as their greatest superpower. But as with any superpower, the hero wielding it needs to know what they can and can't do, what amplifies and diminishes their powers, what the limits of those powers are, and how to use them with purpose.

Here are a few of the definitions that CEOs shared with me on what it means to be a vulnerable leader.

"It means being humble, understanding that nobody has all the answers, including you, and that there is no need to cover this up, change the topic or bully others until you get your point across. This is the opposite of what a good leader does. Be humble and show up in situations as a human being with gaps in knowledge and perspective. Show full acceptance of those things and be open to learning from other people."

—Roel Vestjens, president and CEO, Belden Inc.,
a leading global supplier of digitization and network infrastructure
solutions with more than 8,500 employees

"Vulnerability is about transparency. Sharing what you are doing, why you're doing it, and where your team can play a key role. It's about being transparent and expressing your failures, weaknesses, and insecurities when it's relevant. By doing so your people will appreciate and respect you for it."

—Bill Hornbuckle, president and CEO,
MGM Resorts International, 62,000 employees

"It has everything to do with learning and admitting out loud that you as a leader don't have all the answers. That you are a part of a learning journey where you are pointed toward a better future for the team or organization you are leading."

—Penny Pennington, managing partner
(their term for CEO) of Edward Jones, a *Fortune*
500 financial services firm, 50,000 employees

"It means being open to being wrong; accepting that you need to receive feedback positively and knowing that having the best people around you for decision-making is far stronger than thinking you know everything yourself."

—Lorenzo Simonelli, chairman and CEO,
Baker Hughes, 54,000 employees

"Vulnerable leaders are humble and empathetic people who put mission ahead of ego. They act transparently and embrace feedback. They are driven by a spirit of continuous learning and improvement, and proactively work with mentors, peers, and others to get feedback and learn from it. They seek to understand what truly motivates people, to see through the platitudes and understand what gets people excited about their work."

—Kathy J. Warden, Chair, President & CEO,
Northrop Grumman, 95,000 employees

"What a vulnerable leader means today is very different from what it meant in my earlier years. Vulnerability used to be something you tried to eliminate so you didn't have vulnerable leaders. Today, it's about being who you are and sharing the feelings you have, the struggles you are faced with, and areas you need to improve in. It comes down to connecting with your people and being able to unlock the best in everyone."

—Jim Kavanaugh, CEO and cofounder,
World Wide Technology, 9,000 employees

In my previous book, *The Future Leader*, I interviewed more than 140 CEOs around the world to identify the most important skills and mindsets for current and aspiring leaders. One of the questions I asked these CEOs was to define what it means to be a leader. Based on those responses, I put together the following definition.

A leader is someone who has the ability to see that something can be better than it is now, is able to rally people to move toward that better vision, can come up with a plan to create that vision, and can work toward making that vision a reality while putting people first.

The cover of that book features a lighthouse because that is what leaders represent. As a leader your job is to help your people and your organization achieve their goals and take care of and guide them in the process. Leaders also need to remember that as they build themselves up to be big bright lighthouses, without ships in the water a lighthouse is useless. Meaning that as you learn and grow as a leader, you have to help those around you do the same.

The cover of this book is just as symbolic. Vulnerability is the feeling you get when you can be either emotionally or physically harmed. For the context of this book the physical harm isn't as relevant, but for a few, it may be applicable. The cover features someone getting ready to climb a mountain with a heart-shaped backpack. The symbol of vulnerability is the heart and the mountain is the journey that all leaders must go on. At first the climb will be easy, but then it becomes more challenging. As you stop at various vistas along the way to rest you will meet other people who are on the same journey with you. The higher you climb the more beautiful the view. The farther out you will be able to see, the more clarity you will get, the more connections and relationships you will be able to build with those around you, and the more of an impact you will be able to have. This is an ongoing journey filled with twists and turns, danger and potential loss, but most important, learning, growth, and transformation for yourself and those around you. It's not an easy journey to go on but it's worth it and if you're a leader, it's required.

A vulnerable leader is a leader who intentionally opens himself or herself up to the potential of emotional harm while taking action (when possible) to create a positive outcome. For example, you admit to making a mistake at work and take action to fix it and review what you learned. You share a personal challenge or struggle at work to build trust, connection, and get support. You ask for help and take action to get the necessary training required to get up to speed. The intended outcome is positive. However, as you will see later in the book, a positive outcome is not always the one that occurs. Sometimes we are put in vulnerable situations that we didn't intend to be in. It's how the leader reacts during those times that determines what kind of leader they are. Vulnerability creates connection and leadership is about being good at your job.

When survey participants were asked "What does being a vulnerable leader mean to you?" the top responses were as follows:

- Genuinely asking for help or guidance from others
- Admitting to personal mistakes or failures
- Acknowledging challenges the team or organization is facing
- Acknowledging personal challenges or shortcomings
- Acknowledging when there is risk or uncertainty
- Showing sincere emotions and feelings

You can see the full breakdown in Figure 2.2.

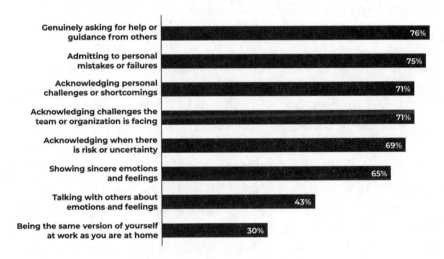

Figure 2.2 What does being vulnerable as a leader mean to you?

These responses were compared across seniority levels, gender, and high-potential versus non-high-potential participants with minimal differences. For example, senior leaders and C-level executives placed "admitting to personal mistakes or failures" as number one instead of number two, and senior leaders also placed "acknowledging personal challenges and shortcomings" as number two instead of number three but the percentage difference was small.

Shockingly, only 16% said their leaders display these qualities of leading with vulnerability often or always when appropriate. This means that most employees around the world work for leaders who don't usually ask for help or guidance from others, admit to personal mistakes or failures, acknowledge challenges the team or organization is facing, acknowledge personal challenges or shortcomings, acknowledge when there is risk or uncertainty, show sincere emotions and feelings, or do any of the other things on the list. This creates an organization where bureaucracy trumps flexibility, the status quo is more important than transformation, title is valued more than trust, compliance is prioritized over innovation, and short-term gains are prioritized over long-term growth. It's a company destined to fail driven by leaders who are more fixated on maintaining their grip on power and immediate profitability than nurturing a future-oriented, resilient organization.

If you don't do these things as a leader, then why would anyone else who works with you do them? More important, would you want to work for a leader who didn't do these things?

We need more vulnerable leaders.

Mindy Grossman is the former CEO of WW International (formerly known as Weight Watchers). She shared a fascinating story with me.

In the 1990s I worked at Ralph Lauren as the president of Chaps. One Friday, I show up to work and get in the elevator along with this gentleman who is the president of the menswear portfolio. The CEO of the company gets in as well and she has her security detail with her. Her office is on the 26th floor and ours is on the 12th. We get in the elevator and the doors close. She then turns to this gentleman and says, "You now report to her," then she turns to me and says, "You now run the whole thing." She also said her secretary would be reaching out to both of us to schedule some time to meet with her. A few hours later, I get a call that Linda, the CEO, wants to meet with me on Saturday at her apartment in the city at 9:00 am. Keep in mind this is all happening on a Friday. My husband had a golf tournament and we had a little child with no babysitter. The following morning, I showed up at the CEO's apartment at 9:00 a.m. with my daughter in a stroller and a tape of Barney. I told her, "This is what it is," and we had our meeting. When I was leaving she told me, "That was bold," and I said, "No, that's called normal," and I left. From that moment I was never again called late at night and I was never asked to work on a weekend.

When I heard this story from Mindy my jaw dropped. There were so many pieces of Mindy's story that I found completely shocking; but it also is a perfect example of vulnerability in the workplace. I couldn't believe how the CEO hired and demoted someone in a six-second elevator ride. This story happened in the 1990s when people were not talking about family leave or workplace wellness. Most people, especially women, swallowed their emotions and white-knuckled their way through harrowing experiences, like having to choose between a career and having a family. And if they made the bold move to try to do both, it got messy. This CEO demanded Mindy show up for work at the boss's house on a Saturday morning without even thinking to ask if Mindy had anything else going on in her life, such as a baby. But for decades this is how companies were led.

I appreciate Mindy's boldness and self-confidence, that she was willing to show up to her boss's house with her baby with no apology, even though she didn't have a babysitter. She held up a reflective mirror to her boss to show her how inappropriate it was for her boss to request her presence on a Saturday morning without having to tell her directly. Mindy was vulnerable and very brave, and it worked for her.

Although vulnerability opens you up to the potential of emotional harm it also opens you up to getting help, learning, growing, and developing yourself and those around you. As Kathy Warden, the president and CEO of Northrop Grumman, shared with me, "The things that make you feel vulnerable are often what make your perspective unique." It's this unique perspective from those around you that enables you to lead through change, and it cannot exist without vulnerability.

Jim Detert is a professor at the University of Virginia and author of *Choosing Courage: The Everyday Guide to Being Brave at Work*. Jim and I spoke fairly late into writing this book, and when I asked him what workplace courage meant, I was shocked by his answer. He defines workplace courage as "an act done for a worthy cause despite significant potential risks."

Wait a minute! That sounds a lot like my definition of being a vulnerable leader!

Through our own independent work we came up with a very similar definition about two different yet related things. It's clear that most people see the connection between vulnerability and courage and oftentimes they are both used in the same sentence. You need courage to be vulnerable but being vulnerable also makes you courageous.

To be a vulnerable leader you need two things: vulnerability and leadership. I call this the Vulnerable Leader Equation, which is shown in Figure 2.3.

VULNERABILITY   LEADERSHIP   LEADING WITH
                                           VULNERABILITY

Figure 2.3   The Vulnerable Leader Equation

$$V \text{ (Vulnerable)} + L \text{ (Leader)}$$
$$= VL \text{ (Leading with Vulnerability)}$$

or

$$V \text{ (Vulnerability)} + L \text{ (Leadership)}$$
$$= VL \text{ (Leading with Vulnerability)}$$

Dr. Susan Fiske, Dr. Amy Cuddy, and Dr. Peter Glick discovered that there are two universal dimensions of social cognition: warmth and competence. Warmth includes elements that are related to perceived intent such as compassion, empathy, trustworthiness, and morality. Competence, however, includes elements that focus on ability such as skill, intelligence, confidence, and creativity.

According to Dr. Fiske, who now teaches at Princeton University, "People have an implicit assumption that if you are competent, then you are not warm, and that if you are highly warm, then you're not competent. In people's minds there's a hydraulic relationship here where if one goes up, the other goes down. However, leaders in today's world need to be both warm and competent."

From my CEO interviews, I discovered that these two dimensions also play a crucial role inside of organizations. Warmth is related to vulnerability and competence is related to leadership; together this is what makes up vulnerable leaders.

Collectively there are eight common attributes of vulnerable leaders, which will be explored more in Chapter 22. Five are for vulnerability and three for leadership. The vulnerable attributes include the following:

- Self-awareness: understanding your thoughts, behaviors, actions, and emotions and how they affect you and those around you
- Self-compassion: being kind to yourself

- Empathy: seeing things from other people's perspectives
- Authenticity: being a single genuine version of yourself
- Integrity: being a moral and honest person with a clear set of personal values that guide how you behave

The leadership attributes include the following:

- Competence: being good at your job
- Self-confidence: belief in yourself and that you have the ability to grow and succeed
- Motivation: the drive to take action and improve

According to Fisk, Cuddy, and Glick's research, they found that warmth is judged before competence. Let's say you join an organization or a new leader is joining your team. The first thing you will pay attention to is their human qualities and characteristics before evaluating if they are good at their job. According to the study's authors, this is because of evolutionary design; another person's intent is at least initially more important than their ability to act on their intentions.

Larry Gies is the CEO and founder of Madison Industries, one of the largest and most successful privately held companies in the world. Here's what he shared: "Teams don't care what you think until they know that you care. You can be the most competent but it will be meaningless to the teams if they don't think you have their back. You can't have their back if you are not vulnerable about the fact that you don't have all the answers and you are not going to risk what you are building together because of your ego. On the other hand, if you are not competent, the team will lose their trust in you and you will not have the ability to be vulnerable."

In DDI's Global Leadership Forecast they identify 13 characteristics of effective manager behaviors, which you can see in Figure 2.4.

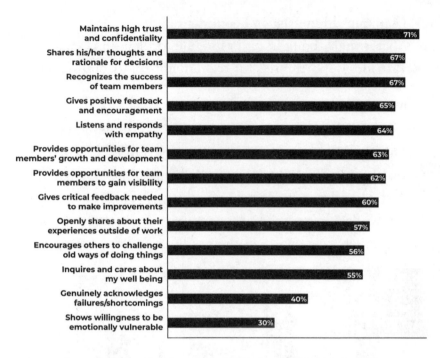

How often does your leader do each of the following (often/always)?

Figure 2.4 Frequency of effective leadership behaviors

These behaviors can be broken down into two types of categories: traditional and emerging. Traditional leadership behaviors are the classic and timeless behaviors that we have always ascribed to leaders, and emerging leadership behaviors are the new behaviors leaders must embrace to lead effectively today and in the future (see Figure 2.5).

Traditional

- Recognizes the success of team members
- Gives critical feedback needed to make improvements
- Gives positive feedback and encouragement
- Provides opportunities for team members' growth and development

- Maintains high trust and confidentiality
- Shares their thoughts and rationale for decisions
- Provides opportunities for team members to gain visibility

Emerging

- Encourages others to challenge old ways of doing things
- Openly shares about their experiences outside of work
- Inquires and cares about my well-being
- Listens and responds with empathy
- Shows a willingness to be vulnerable
- Genuinely acknowledges their failures and shortcomings

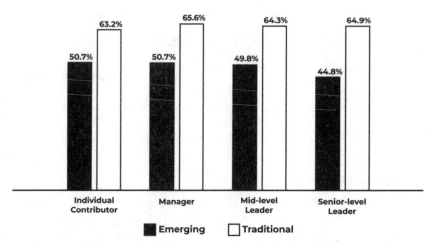

Figure 2.5   Frequency of emerging versus traditional leadership behaviors

It's not a coincidence that across the board leaders practice traditional behaviors far more often than the emerging ones, which include vulnerability and more of the "human" behaviors. In Figure 2.5 you can see that after "manager" the more senior you become the less likely you are to practice emerging leadership behaviors. Not only that but the gap between traditional and emerging behaviors grows substantially, especially when someone becomes a senior-level leader.

Looking at the data it's clear that inside of organizations around the world we prioritize the traditional leadership behaviors while we underappreciate the value and the impact that the emerging "human" behaviors can have. In fact, when breaking this down a bit further, senior leaders scored lowest in showing a willingness to be vulnerable (13%), genuinely acknowledging failure or shortcomings (26%), and inquiring and caring about the well-being of others (39%) (see Figure 2.6).

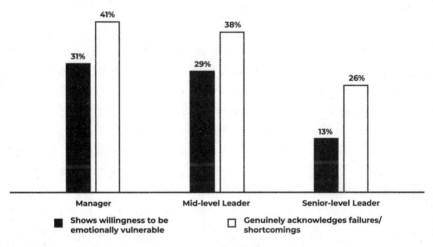

Figure 2.6 Frequency of leadership behavior by level (often/always)

Based on these two factors of vulnerability and leadership there are four types of leaders: the novice, robot, incompetent leader, and vulnerable leader (see Figure 2.7).

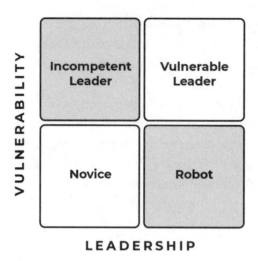

Figure 2.7   Four types of leaders

The novice is either someone who is new in their leadership journey or someone who isn't a leader yet. Therefore they have not yet established their leadership or vulnerability. The path they take here will determine what kind of a leader they end up as.

The robot is someone who is effective in leadership yet struggles with vulnerability. These can be thought of as more stereotypical leaders who got to where they are by focusing more on competence instead of connection.

The incompetent leader is someone who is vulnerable yet struggles with leadership. Perhaps this leader was once quite competent but then stopped learning and growing after becoming a leader. Another possibility is that this person became a leader simply by navigating through office politics and bureaucracy. They are good at the human aspects of work but should not be in a position where they are leading others.

The vulnerable leader is someone who combines the elements of vulnerability and leadership to achieve positive change and outcomes. These are the leaders who are both good at their jobs and can connect with their people on a human level. There are five types of vulnerable leaders that you will discover later in the book.

Remember that anyone can become a vulnerable leader because today you need both vulnerability and leadership to be successful.

Most of the literature and research out there does not address the potential of leadership when vulnerability is approached in the right way. In the upcoming pages I illustrate what has worked and what the research says will work for you in the future. Inside of organizations it's clear that vulnerability alone is not enough to achieve the desired outcomes of the individuals, the team, or the business. Vulnerability is not always a good thing at work, especially if you are not highly competent at your job. Vulnerability for leaders is not the same as it is for everyone else.

Figure 2.8 compares the differences between being vulnerable versus being a vulnerable leader. We don't need more vulnerability at work; we need more vulnerable leadership.

VULNERABLE	VULNERABLE LEADER
Admitting to a mistake	Admitting to a mistake (V) and sharing what was learned (L).
Asking for help	Asking for help (V) and committing to learning what you need help with (L).
Showing emotion	Showing emotion (V) but practicing self-awareness to be conscientious of how that emotion comes across and the impact it can have (L).
Saying "I don't know"	Saying "I don't know" (V) but having an idea or a plan for how to figure it out (L).
Talking about personal challenges or struggles	Talking about personal challenges or struggles (V) for the purpose of connecting, creating trust and relatability, as opposed to a therapy session (L).
Being unsure	Being unsure (V) but having a vision for where you want to end up (L).

Figure 2.8 Being vulnerable compared to being a vulnerable leader

Do you see the difference? Vulnerable leaders have to take that extra step of adding the L (Leadership).

Brad Jackson is the cofounder and CEO of Slalom, a consulting firm with more than 13,000 employees. He put this nicely: "Vulnerability by itself is not enough. It's like hydrogen, which by itself can do some really great things. But when you combine it with leadership where there is a focus on outcome, reflection, and trust, that's when its true power becomes unleashed and it can 100× your organization, it can change your life, and change the lives of hundreds, maybe even millions."

Vulnerable leaders understand three truths:

- Leading from a place of connection and influence is more powerful than leading from a place of fear or compliance. Compliance checks things off a to-do list; connection and influence can change the world.
- The opposite of being vulnerable is not invulnerable; it's stagnation and eventual decline. You cannot learn and grow without vulnerability.
- The combination of vulnerability and leadership will transform you, your team, and your organization. It will unlock your true potential and the true potential of those around you.

Anyone has the power to combine leadership and vulnerability, including you. Whether you are a CEO or an entry-level employee, one of the best things you can do for yourself and your teams' success is practice the concept of V + L = VL.

3

Why Lead with Vulnerability?

What It Means to You

We all know and have worked with leaders who are the farthest thing from being vulnerable. Yet somehow they are still leaders. They have the authority, salary, equity, benefits, office, and great parking spot. Many leaders got their role because they are good at navigating office politics, they know someone who helped get them promoted, they have been at the company for a long time, they help make the company money, or perhaps they are just good business operators.

So if they didn't have to be vulnerable to get to their position, why should you?

To answer this question, we turn to the Edith checkerspot butterfly.[1] Nevada was home to a particular species of butterfly called the Edith checkerspot. These butterflies had a favorite plant to lay eggs on called the blue-eyed Mary. For many years the butterflies thrived until one day humans came into the area and brought cattle along with them. But with the cattle came an invasive new plant called ribwort plantain, which took over the blue-eyed Mary.

Gradually, the butterflies were able to adapt to this new plant and even thrived until 2005 when the humans abruptly left and took their cattle with them. Without the cattle grazing in the fields, the grass grew and covered the ribwort plantain so that butterflies couldn't land on it to lay eggs or eat. Unfortunately, the butterflies had already adapted to this new plant and abandoned their dependency on the blue-eyed Mary. As a result, all of the Edith checkerspot butterflies died. (The story has a happy ending, though, as over the next four years butterflies from other meadows who didn't abandon the blue-eyed Mary came back to repopulate the area.)

Mismatch theory is an explanation for what happens when traits or behaviors that were once advantageous become detrimental as a result of a changing environment.[2] In the case of the Edith checkerspot, the butterflies became dependent on the ribwort plantain and were not able to adapt when their environment suddenly changed.

This is what is happening to leaders and leadership today. For decades we have collectively become dependent on leadership stereotypes and on the notion that vulnerability is weakness. In fact, *Fortune* used to have an annual list of the toughest bosses and making it to that list was considered a badge of honor as was working for one of the CEOs on the list.

In an issue from the 1990s titled "Seven CEOs Who Make Your Top Dog Look Like a Pussycat," the magazine wrote, "T. J. Rodgers, head of Cypress Semiconductor, puts on what he calls a 'drooling psycho face' to harangue employees." They also quote Linda Wachner, the CEO of Warnaco and the only CEO of a *Fortune* 500 company at the time as telling an employee, "You'd better start firing people so they'll understand you're serious." Another CEO, Jack Connors, from the ad agency Hill, Holliday, Connors, Cosmopulos, was described as flying into rages that employees called "Jack attacks." Not surprisingly, Jack Welch, the former CEO of GE, also made the list. He was nicknamed Neutron Jack for eliminating employees while leaving the buildings standing, just like a neutron bomb. You know who else made that list? Harvey Weinstein.[3]

Can you imagine if this list still existed today? The list might not exist but the outdated approaches to leadership still do. Leadership is not about being in control; it's about being vulnerable enough to let others take control when they need to. You cannot lead others if you do not let others lead you.

Nancy McKinstry is the CEO and chair of the executive board at Wolters Kluwer, a Dutch-based, global leader in professional information, software solutions, and services with about 20,000 employees worldwide. She recounted what it was like in business school in the 1980s, which also extended well into the 1990s and is still quite prevalent inside of today's schools and organizations:

> I was in business school when Jack Welch was at his pinnacle of success. Vulnerable leadership was not what they taught in business school. It was much more of being a celebrity CEO, although, of course, it wasn't framed that way. It was all about centralized control, command-and-control, and military-style leadership. There was no vulnerability, emotion, or weakness; that was all discouraged. This is the type of leadership that was taught to me and at the time it didn't seem odd at all because it was the phase of business we were all in. Of course, this has changed dramatically and I and many other leaders had to unlearn and learn what it means to be a leader, but many of those outdated practices and approaches are still inside of organizations today.

Just like with the Edith checkerspot butterfly, our environment has suddenly changed. Employee experience has become a top talent priority, shareholder value has been replaced by stakeholder value, employee well-being has taken center stage, we are dealing with the aftermaths of COVID and a turbulent geopolitical climate, purpose and meaning are becoming more important than profits and money, and the collective business mindset has shifted toward actually putting people first.

Unfortunately, we are still reliant on outdated ways of leading and thinking about vulnerability and our once useful leadership traits and behaviors are now causing us harm.

Jason McGowan is the founder and CEO of Crumbl Cookies, which has more than 30,000 team members. When we spoke, he told me that vulnerability is the great unifier for his organization, which I thought was a unique take: "Everyone has a unique sense of the truth in their head. Our team members might have an idea around how they should work, how the company should operate, what the employee and employer relationship should look like, or how we can best serve customers. Without vulnerability everyone operates in their own reality. As a leader, when you are vulnerable by doing something like asking for help or talking about a challenge you bring everyone together into a single reality. This is what allows for leading through change and growth and progress on both an individual and corporate level."

Leading with vulnerability creates both truth and trust. It enables you to bring team members to a common understanding where individuals have each other's backs and best interests at heart.

Do you need to be a vulnerable leader? Well, it depends. Do you want to take the risk of relying on outdated ways of leading as the environment around you changes in the hopes that maybe nobody will notice? Or do you want to adapt to the environment you're in so you can lead and make a positive impact on those around you?

Unfortunately, 81% of leaders have not been equipped with the tools or training to be vulnerable in an effective way. Considering that vulnerability is a part of being human and that we want our organizations to be more human, this is a staggeringly high number.

If you are a current or aspiring leader who wants to have a successful leadership career, then it's time to think differently. Our world has changed; you need to change with it.

What It Means to the Business

Michael McGarry is the executive chairman and former CEO of PPG, one of the world's largest paints, coatings, and materials companies with more than 50,000 employees. In October 2018, activist investor Nelson Peltz, who owned $690 million dollars of PPG stock, put out a whitepaper saying that the company needed to be split and that he as the CEO needed to be fired. The story made headlines across major media outlets.

> As you can imagine this was a very uncomfortable position for me and there isn't a playbook on how to deal with someone publicly calling you out to get fired. I had to be vulnerable and ask for help and guidance from other CEOs and board members who had experience with this sort of thing. Of course, I was also questioning myself as a leader and the strategies I had been implementing at the company. I received guidance and advice from others and then rejected Nelson's proposal to have me removed and the company split. I was backed unanimously by my team. Asking for help and being vulnerable doesn't make you weak; it makes you a strong leader and had I not asked for help I likely would not have remained as CEO.

What's the impact of leading with vulnerability to your business? When leaders in companies frequently display vulnerability when appropriate, employees are 5.7× more likely to rate the quality of leadership as very good or excellent than companies who rarely or never display vulnerability, and the percentage of leaders considered high quality increases by 37% on average.

Tony Sarsam is the CEO of SpartanNash, a food solutions company with more than 175,000 associates. He does a good job of connecting vulnerability to being human: "Everyone who works at SpartanNash shares things in common. We all have hopes and fears, successes, and aspirations. We have broken-down cars, failed marriages or relationships, families, and pets. We all have various endeavors as we go through our life journey and we all know what ups and downs feel like. People take comfort in knowing that when they work here, this isn't a sterile environment. This is a place where people can be human beings, which means being vulnerable. This is the only business justification I need: for people to feel like they are human."

We are all vulnerable whether we choose to recognize it and accept it or not. At this very moment you are in a vulnerable situation with someone in your professional or personal life and you have shared something with someone who can use that information to harm you. It's not possible to exist without feeling and being vulnerable.

I love how Amy Edmondson put this:

We are all operating in an uncertain, complex, and volatile world. Nobody has a crystal ball or a magic wand. This means we are all vulnerable to harm from external events we don't anticipate. Vulnerability is therefore a fact. The only question is whether you recognize and are willing to acknowledge it. There's wisdom in knowing you're vulnerable and acknowledging it. When you do this, you're better prepared to handle the risks that uncertainty and complexity bring. When leaders are up-front about their vulnerability, others are more willing to speak up and step up to address the challenges that lie ahead.

Being vulnerable is not a requirement for mediocrity but it is a prerequisite for great leadership. If you simply care about getting employees to accomplish their tasks, crossing things off of your to-do list, and maintaining the status quo, then you don't need to be a vulnerable leader.

Based on the survey data, employees of managers who regularly display vulnerability when appropriate are able to do the following:

- 1.7× more likely to develop novel ideas or solutions (innovate)
- 2.7× more likely to allow themselves to be vulnerable with others at work
- 5.3× more likely to trust their manager

Additionally, manager vulnerability affects employees' feelings of trust toward senior leaders as well. When their manager regularly displays vulnerability, employees are 2.2× more likely to say they trust their senior leaders to do what is right. Vulnerable leaders also have a tremendous impact on employee engagement. When leaders frequently display vulnerability, their direct reports are 2.9× more likely to be engaged in their roles in comparison to those whose organizations rarely or never display vulnerability.

Mark S. Hoplamazian is the president and CEO of Hyatt Hotels Corporation with more than 164,000 employees globally. We had a great discussion about this and here's something he shared with me:

> Early in my career, I learned that my title of CEO may get you compliance but it doesn't do anything to help you connect with other people. That's something you have to work hard on. I never want people to do something because they know it's from the CEO but because they know it's the right direction for us to go in and it's my job to help them along that path. The only way you can lead from connection and not from compliance is when people don't see you as your title but they see you as a real person with a job to do and as someone they can relate to. People need to understand you in human terms, not hierarchical terms, which is why being a vulnerable leader is so important. It allows you to lead from a place of connection and being human.

The survey data also revealed that when leaders in an organization display vulnerability regularly, leaders are twice as likely to plan to stay in their organizations within the next year compared to those who belong to organizations whose leaders do not display vulnerability.

If you want to connect with human beings, transform lives, grow, and develop yourself and those around you, create a legacy, unlock potential, discover new opportunities, solve complex problems, grow your team and business, and make a positive impact, you will not be able to do that without vulnerability.

Milind Pant is the CEO of Amway, which has more than 15,000 employees around the world. Vulnerability is the core of how he leads and how his company operates: "Our organization and our culture flourishes when we are leading from the heart. This especially has to come from me and our leaders. If I don't walk the talk, then how will we be able to nourish this culture? We are in the people business, and we have over a million entrepreneurs around the world. Our relationship with them is the most important thing in the world. Being vulnerable creates those relationships and it's who we hire, how we grow, and how we have achieved success."

Being a vulnerable leader is about leading from a place of connection, influence, and relationships, as opposed to leading from a place of power. As you heard from Mark Hoplamazian, leading from a place of power and authority gets you compliance but nothing more. Purely focusing on compliance is a death sentence for any organization and the careers of the leaders who run them. Compliance doesn't create growth or innovation, compliance doesn't unlock new opportunities, compliance doesn't create better customer or employee experiences. Compliance doesn't unlock the potential of people and it doesn't enable you to lead through change. Compliance keeps you right where you are and then slowly strangles you.

This means that as a leader you have to acknowledge that your role in your company and who you are as a person are not the same thing. Compliance comes from your position; connection and influence come from who you are as a person. Compliance is for the status quo, connection is for leading through change. If you transition to work for another company, someone else will have your position and will be able to exert the same level of compliance. But you take your ability to lead from connection and influence wherever you go.

Thomas Gayner is the CEO of Markel, a holding company for insurance, reinsurance, and investment operations with more than 20,000 employees. He understands the power of leading with vulnerability:

> There are times when I see things differently than those around me. I might be aware of something that others are not and vice versa. This means that alone, nobody has a clear picture of what is going on and no single person can make the best decision. To get that clear picture and to make the best decisions, leaders have to bring in different perspectives and ideas from their people. If those around you are scared to speak up, to share their struggles or challenges, or to talk about who they are as human beings, then they will never really share their ideas and perspectives with you. Leaders cannot possibly be effective without vulnerability.

It turns out that the more often leaders lead with vulnerability the higher quality those leaders are perceived to be. The relationship is crystal clear, and as you can see in Figure 3.1, it is very significant that in organizations where vulnerability is displayed rarely or not at all, only 56% of those leaders are perceived as high quality compared to 86% of leaders who are perceived as high quality in organizations where vulnerability is displayed always (again, when the time calls for it). That's a massive 30% difference. Leading with vulnerability is a game changer.

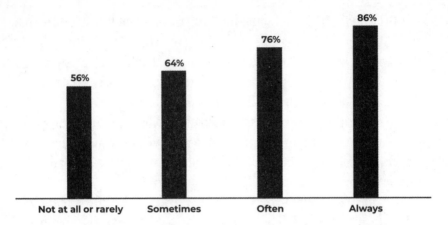

Do leaders at your organization display vulnerability?

Figure 3.1   Percentage of high-quality leaders in organizations

Every CEO I interviewed clearly saw the return on investment (ROI) of leading with vulnerability. Julie Godin, the co-chair of the board at CGI, a 90,000-person consulting firm, is one of those leaders. "The ROI of vulnerable leadership is employee engagement. After I started being vulnerable, I heard from other leaders who felt empowered to do the same. When leaders do this, it allows employees to be vulnerable as well. It empowers employees to take risks, to share ideas, and to aim big without fear of being reprimanded if they fail. In our company, we also clearly see how vulnerable leadership has impacted employee retention, which is consistently higher than our industry peers."

But if you need more data, organizations regularly displaying vulnerability are 4.5× more likely to be prepared to foster an inclusive culture at work than those who do not. They are also 2.3× more likely to feel prepared to operate in a highly ambiguous business environment and 2.4× more likely to be prepared to manage a remote workforce. Additionally, when leaders at organizations display vulnerability regularly, leaders are twice as likely to report feeling prepared to engage and retain top talent as those who belong to organizations that do not. This has huge implications because retaining top talent and maintaining an engaged workforce are two of the most frequently cited concerns as identified by CEOs in the DDI Global Leadership Forecast.

Marek Piechocki is the founder and CEO of LPP, the largest fashion company in Eastern and Central Europe with more than 30,000 employees. He understands this concept clearly. "The success of my people is also my success, but their failure is also my personal failure. I'm always asking myself what I can do to protect those who work with and for me while at the same time recognize them for their wins. I depend on and appreciate all of the people I work with and understand that without them there would be no company. I remind myself of that every day and that guides why and how I lead with vulnerability."

Whenever I try to understand a concept or an idea, I try to imagine something that represents it. When it comes to leading with vulnerability, the visual I keep coming back to is islands. Each human being is their own island and we're all just floating around the world. If we want to visit another island or connect with it somehow, then we need to build a bridge to get to that island. Vulnerability is the bridge. As a leader, you can command the island in your company and tell them what to do and how to do it, but you will never build that bridge and connection with them unless you are vulnerable.

Kathy Mazzarella is the chairman, president, and CEO of Graybar, a supply chain management services company with more than 8,800 employees. She told me, "Vulnerability helps deepen human connections throughout your organization. Of course, being vulnerable helps others trust you as a leader. It helps you relate to them, shows that you care, and gives them confidence in you and your intentions. When people have confidence in you as a leader, it builds confidence in the organization, its vision, and its strategy. Vulnerability contributes to high-trust team environments, which allows everyone to be their best every day."

There are lots of people in the world who are quite successful despite not having to be vulnerable, I was one of them! Regardless of what you believe, there will be times in your life when you will have to be vulnerable whether you want to be or not. At some point or another, life will make you vulnerable. But for most people, when vulnerability is forced on them unexpectedly, they don't know how to react or what to do and as a result they have a hard time overcoming whatever challenge they are faced with.

$N + 1$

If you look at your computer, your phone, or any other piece of technology that is running software on it, you will find a version number. Typically every few months a new version of that software is released with new updates and features, but all of that software at some point started at the very beginning, which we can call N and with each release it becomes $N + 1$, where that new number becomes N and then again we have $N + 1$.

Aart de Geus is the chairman and CEO of Synopsys, a 20,000-person technology company he co-founded over 35 years ago. He's been thinking about vulnerability for a long time, but he approaches it in terms of version $n + 1$ ($Vn + 1$). I like this idea because we forget that we are always iterations of ourselves. We continue to evolve all the time. You are not the same person you were one year ago, and you will not be the person you are right now in five years.

A few years ago, I created a YouTube video that explored a similar concept. I said we needed to view ourselves like apps that keep getting upgraded with new features and abilities.

Here's how Aart explains it.

The first thing you have to accept is that you are not perfect and you want to improve and get better. It could be a small gradual change with $Vn + 1$ or it can be a huge breakthrough with $Vn + 500$! If you aren't vulnerable in accepting and sharing that you can improve, then how can you get better? By not being vulnerable you signal that you are perfect, which is not true. Leaders need to remember never to confuse the person with the position, but many lead from the virtue of the position that they achieve instead of the person they are. The danger for many leaders is to avoid a situation where this turns into a $Vn - 1$ or $Vn - 500$ situation. In this case, you are either moving backwards or perhaps you are staying where you are, but the world is moving ahead of you, which makes you $Vn - 1$ by default. The aspiration is to continuously learn, grow, and develop as a leader. You will never be a $Vn +$ version of yourself without vulnerability.

By thinking of yourself as an app it forces you to ask how you can keep learning, growing, and getting better. The past few years have forced all of us to confront an unparalleled level of uncertainty. The best and only way to lead in that kind of an environment is to bring people together, explore new ideas, learn and grow, create trust, and unlock the potential of those around you. Leading with vulnerability is how you lead through change. As Aart pointed out this is not possible unless you are willing to be vulnerable and it requires changing your mindset on how you view vulnerability.

Steve Fisher is the president and CEO of Novelis, an aluminum company with more than 13,000 employees. He is one of the leaders who has changed how he thinks about vulnerability. "There is an assumption that red on a scorecard is negative. But this just identifies where the opportunities are. As a leader, there is nothing wrong with being vulnerable and acknowledging where you are struggling and challenged as long as you see those things as opportunities to improve and help others do the same."

This is the Vulnerable Leader Equation in action.

Vulnerability, Trust, and Interdependence

A common theme that emerged from all of my CEO interviews, when I asked them why anyone should bother becoming a vulnerable leader, was trust. When there is trust inside of an organization employees share new ideas, are more comfortable talking about mistakes and failures, and are more engaged in the work they do. When their manager regularly displays vulnerability, employees are 2.2× more likely to say they trust their senior leaders to do what is right. Trust plays a crucial role in our lives and in our organizations, but there is no trust without vulnerability.

Joel Quadracci is the chairman, president, and CEO of Quad, a $3 billion global marketing experience company. The 51-year-old company grew up as a commercial printer and had to reinvent itself several times over the years. How can you have reinvention like this without acknowledging that the business is changing, that the future is uncertain, and that as a leader you don't have all of the answers? You can't.

> In the situations where the buck stops with me, I feel very vulnerable. If I charge up the wrong hill, it's not just the lives of the 15,000 employees that I impact, but also their families. As the CEO I'm responsible for all of them. Because I'm vulnerable with my team and talk about my challenges, mistakes, and where I need help, they trust me. This means that they can come to me with their best ideas, criticisms, opportunities, and risks. As the CEO, sometimes it feels like for three-quarters of the year I run on fear and for one-quarter it's this feeling of "Okay, it's working." In today's world, companies can appear or disappear in the blink of an eye. When I feel like the weight of the world is on my shoulders, I turn to my team because they get me to think differently and see things from perspectives that I never thought of. Ultimately, this helps me make the best decisions for the company and everyone involved. It comes back to vulnerability and trust.

One of the world's leading experts on all things trust is Dr. Sim Sitkin. He's a professor of leadership management and public policy at Duke's Fuqua School of Business, where he is also the faculty director of the Fuqua/Coach K Center on Leadership & Ethics and director of the Behavioral Science and Policy Center. He's been studying and writing about trust longer than I've been alive.

In a paper he coauthored with Denise M. Rousseau, Ronald S. Burt, and Colin Camerer, "Not So Different After All: A Cross-Discipline View of Trust," they found that there are 22 definitions of *trust* in academic literature, and they all have to do with making yourself vulnerable.

The definition of trust Dr. Sitkin and his colleagues came up with is "trust is a psychological state comprising the intention to accept vulnerability based upon positive expectations of the intentions or behavior of another."

Trust is the willingness to be vulnerable and take a risk when interacting with others, while also holding a positive and optimistic expectation of their actions. It requires courage and a willingness to potentially be hurt, but it is essential in building strong relationships. Trust is built on the understanding that mistakes will be made and vulnerability is accepted. Trust built on the expectation of perfection is a house of cards as it disregards the humanity of those involved.

Once again, we see the relationship among vulnerability, workplace courage, and now trust (see Figure 3.2).

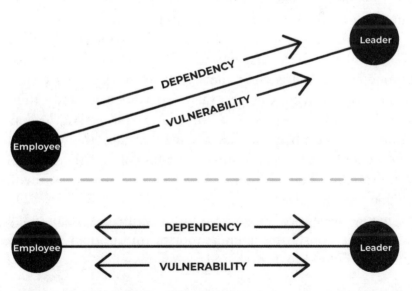

Figure 3.2 Level the playing field

How does vulnerability help you lead through change? Inside of organizations there is an interdependency that needs to be acknowledged and plays a critical role in trust and vulnerability. As a leader, when individuals work for you, they may feel a sense of vulnerability due to the power and authority you hold over them. You can fire them, demote them, move them to another team, or make their life at work hell. Why would they want to put themselves at risk of having any of those things happen to them? Your people depend on you to keep them safe, help them learn and grow, and have their back; as a result they are vulnerable to you.

However, there is also an interdependency that flows the opposite direction from leaders to employees. Leaders depend on their employees to do things such as come up with ideas, service customers, close deals, make strategic business decisions, push back when they think the leader is making a mistake, and get work done in the right way. Everyone around you right now is there because of a choice they made. They get a paycheck and benefits to be there but nobody is forcing them to stay; they are not prisoners, and it's voluntary. You need the creativity, hard work, ingenuity, collaboration, vision, and passion of those around you so that the business can succeed.

The big difference is that in the first scenario the vulnerability and dependency between employee and leader is one that everyone knows and is clear about. But in the second scenario leaders rarely acknowledge their dependency and their vulnerability to their people. According to Dr. Sitkin, leaders become risk averse because they assume that they are in control of their people and circumstances. The outcome is that leaders end up thinking that, although their teams need to trust them, they don't need to trust their teams.

Thierry Delaporte is the CEO of Wipro, a technology services and consulting company with more than 255,000 employees. Here's what he shared with me:

Historically, vulnerability has never been encouraged, nor expected from those in leadership positions. It is somewhat of a given that the more senior you are, the more fortitude and endurance you must display. Perhaps even stoicism! But imagine a scenario if one day everyone in the firm decided to leave. You will be left with nothing, because you will have no one to lead. It's like being a lighthouse without ships to guide. I think leaders must acknowledge the fundamental truth that they too can be vulnerable and dependent on others, both at work and at home. That openness and environment of trust and vulnerability is what makes a great team and a great company. Vulnerability—like trust and respect—is a two-way street.

As a leader there is vulnerability when you recognize and appreciate that there is a dependency on those you work with. By being vulnerable and telling your people, "I can't do this without you," you can create a level playing field and foster an environment in which your team members feel comfortable sharing their own thoughts and ideas. This is ultimately what leads to the creation of trust, engagement, innovation, and productivity. These are all critical elements that are required to lead through change of any kind. Without them, you simply have compliance, which only works in environments based on the status quo.

Dr. Sitkin's advice for leaders is to lead by example and absorb the risk of being vulnerable because you are in a powerful position and can afford to do so. This means that if an idea works, leaders should give credit to their teams, and if something fails, leaders need to be the ones absorbing the hits and taking the blame. Unfortunately, what happens in most organizations is the exact opposite. Leaders want to preserve and protect their stature, perception, and power instead of leveraging it to help others and create trust through vulnerability. In fact, one of the ways leaders avoid being vulnerable in terms of team dynamics is they avoid hiring people who are better, more talented, or more capable than they are.

In a telling study, Dr. Craig Fox and his team at UCLA put together a list of words that tend to be associated with knowable uncertainty (where you can calculate a probability), such as *assess*, *presume*, and *model*. They also put together a list of words associated with random uncertainty (where you can't calculate a probability), such as *chance*, *black swan*, and *distribution*. They then looked at the publicly available transcripts of earnings announcements of major companies. It turns out that when a company's earnings exceed analysts' forecasts, the company talks about it as if it was predictable and knowable. But when a company falls short, they talk about it in terms of chance. Meaning, leaders of organizations want the credit when things go well but they don't want to show vulnerability when things don't go well, instead trying to shield themselves from mistakes or failure by saying it was just bad luck.

Sterling Nielsen is the president and CEO of Mountain America Credit Union with more than 3,000 employees. I love what he told me about this:

> If my organization is going to be successful, I'm going to need great people around me. The best way to attract and retain the very best is to give them a meaningful position where they can make a difference, where they can develop other leaders, where they can make decisions on their own, and not have to ask permission every step of the way, where they contribute to the overall success of the organization. Being a vulnerable leader allows you to do that and to let go and let the experts make the call on decisions. It allows people to trust each other to make important calls and allows them to make mistakes. It also forced me as a leader to be vulnerable enough to say "there's a better way of doing things."

If you as a leader want to be able to trust others and have others in turn trust you, then it's not possible to do that without vulnerability being a part of the equation. Research also shows that trust begets trust—if I want you to trust me and take my interests into account, one of the ways of encouraging that is for me to show that I trust you, even though we both know you could take advantage of that trust.

As Dr. Sitkin framed it during our interview, "You need to ask yourself, 'Why don't I have the strength and self-confidence to allow others to shine or to take the risk of being dependent on them for our mutual success?'" It takes a certain amount of courage to be willing to accept those risks (of not being the best, or of being personally accountable when others have made a mistake under your authority). Even though you may be the boss, this means to some extent you are dependent on those you lead— and therein lies the risk and vulnerability. Sometimes those risks are big and require heroic courage and other times they are more ordinary and involve what Sitkin and Moran Anisman-Razin refer to as "everyday courage."

Steve McMillan is the CEO of Teradata, a 7,000-person cloud analytics and data company. He attributes vulnerability to his success: "Vulnerability is what creates human connection and allows leaders to support diverse populations in the workforce. When you're vulnerable you become less intimidating and more relatable—which for leaders is absolutely crucial. In fact, vulnerability has been a key part of my success, being true to myself. This shows up in all of my relationships and creates trust and connection, which is like air and water for leaders. As trust increases, communication increases, innovation increases, and the speed of action inside the company increases."

Trust inevitably involves a certain amount of courage because it involves both risk and vulnerability. Dr. Sitkin told me that it's this stereotype of leadership that is considered to be the ticket to entry, and that once you get a leadership role, people assume you are competent and confident but what those around you want to know now is, are you also human . . . and that's where vulnerability comes in.

Inside most organizations, leaders (and all of us for that matter) assume that trust needs to be earned. But one of the best things you can do is trust by default. In other words, start off with trust and don't force people to earn it. Instead, give people the opportunity to prove why you shouldn't trust them. You will find that this won't happen very often. One of the ways you can do this is—you guessed it—be vulnerable.

If you lead with vulnerability and it does get used against you, it's because the person, the team, the culture, or the environment isn't one that supports or encourages it, and you should ask yourself if that is a person, team, or company you want to be connected with. I think we all know the answer to that question.

George Oliver is the chairman and CEO of Johnson Controls, a company with more than 100,000 employees that specializes in creating smart, healthy, and sustainable buildings. Here's what he shared with me: "Over time I realized that everything I do is built on the foundation of relationships, which is based on trust and respect. When you get into tough situations, the more you can be yourself, be open, transparent, and vulnerable, the more you can build those relationships and create trust, the stronger those relationships will be. This is the only way to achieve something that is sustainable and will last over the long term."

It's clear from the many CEO quotes and stories in this section that the forward-thinking leaders see clear value in leading with vulnerability, and you should, too. The opposite of being vulnerable is not invulnerable; it's stagnation and eventual decline.

Being a vulnerable leader is the most powerful person you can become to unlock potential in others, lead through change, and to transform your company. It might not be comfortable or easy for you with your background and experience, but it's something we can all learn, and being a vulnerable leader is someone we can all become.

If you as a leader want to be able to trust others and have others in turn trust you to be able to pursue learning and to try new things, then it's not possible to do that without vulnerability being a part of the equation. Vulnerability is all about ambiguity, uncertainty, and putting yourself in a situation where you can lose something, all things we try to avoid.[4] This shows just how hard vulnerability can be and why it requires courage.

As a leader, this is your privilege and your responsibility to the people you lead.

4

Tough Guys

When he was 14 years old, Tommy Chreene started working on oil rigs in the Gulf of Mexico for Shell. It was an exciting job that he loved, but it was also a dangerous job where people lost their lives. In an interview he did for NPR in 2016, accompanied by a brilliant article they published, he recounted a story of how he saw one such tragedy occur.

One man had just finished his shift and was standing in front of a massive pipe that workers had twisted into the ground. It was held in place with a handle that the man accidentally kicked, which caused all of the tension to release. As it swung around it caught the man's ankle and whipped him around. As Tommy recounts, "In about three seconds, it spun him around about 80 times," A few feet from the man was a post, and "his head was hitting that post like a rotten tomato."

Tommy and his team were given 15 minutes to mourn the death of their colleague and then had to get back to work.

Even in the face of death, the men on the oil rig never showed any vulnerability. If they needed help, they didn't ask. If they felt they couldn't do a job, they stayed quiet and did it anyway. If they felt burned out or unhappy, they put up a façade.

Sounds like many corporate environments today, doesn't it?

In most organizations we don't ask for help because we don't want to look weak, we don't challenge or question our leaders because we don't want to get in trouble, and we don't show emotion because it's not something that leaders do. It's expected that we just show up to work each day, keep our heads down, and do what is asked of us—like robots. The problem is we're human.

In 1997, Shell started building the world's deepest offshore oil rig, called Ursa. It was more than 48 stories tall and cost almost $1.5 billion.

Overseeing this project as the asset manager for Ursa was Rick Fox. He was aware of the high incidents of injury and death on oil rigs and with Ursa, the levels of risk were even higher. Rick understood that if Ursa was going to be a success in terms of construction and operation, then something had to change.

One day Rick got a call from a woman named Claire Neur, a leadership consultant and holocaust survivor. She had heard about the challenges of building the world's deepest offshore oil rig with Ursa and said she could help Rick and his team.

Over the next 18 months, Rick and his team of more than 100 oil rig workers came to Shell's headquarters in New Orleans to participate in workshops and sessions designed to create a safe environment for vulnerability. These were all-day sessions starting at 6 a.m. and oftentimes ending at 11 p.m.

At first there was hesitation and apprehension, and some of the men didn't understand what any of this had to do with an oil rig. But eventually the men started to share things about their families and lives. Some men talked about their failed relationships and parents who were alcoholics; others talked about growing up in poverty; Tommy, who had one of the biggest "tough guy" reputations, talked about his son with a terminal illness and began "weeping like a baby" in front of the other men.

One of the men was George Horn, who said of the workshops, "It felt vulnerable. You put your personal life out there for everybody to hear and everybody to see."

The sessions forced these macho men to be open with their feelings. The workshops allowed them to talk about their mistakes and challenges and ask for help. As a result, they completely changed how they communicated with one another.

According to an article published by *The Harvard Business Review* called "Unmasking Manly Men" by Robin J. Ely and Debra Meyerson, "the accident rate plummeted by 84% while productivity (number of barrels produced), efficiency (cost per barrel), and reliability (production "up" time) increased beyond the industry's previous benchmark."[1]

The authors said, "The people who used to rise to the top— the "biggest, baddest roughnecks," as one worker described them—weren't necessarily the best at improving safety and effectiveness. Rather, the ones who excelled were mission-driven guys who cared about their fellow workers, were good listeners, and were willing to learn." These men became better fathers, sons, friends, partners, team members, and human beings.

If men working on oil rigs became comfortable sharing how they're feeling and talking about their challenges and struggles, then I believe we can create a culture of vulnerable leaders inside of organizations around the world. Going to 16-hour-long group therapy sessions and sharing the details of your personal life aren't requirements for leading with vulnerability, but being a human being is.

In May 2014, James Fish was at the Barclay offices in New York City surrounded by some of the world's toughest lawyers, negotiators, and business executives. At the time James was the CFO of Waste Management, and he was negotiating a multibillion-dollar sale of the business to private equity. All the people in the room wanted to tear James to pieces.

His mom was sick in Austin, Texas, and he was skeptical about leaving her, but she encouraged him to go, saying that she knew how important this deal was and that she would be there when he got back. So James flew to New York, where he spent several days locked in a conference room from 7 a.m. until 10 p.m. at night. In the middle of one of these tough negotiations, James saw that his twin sister called and he knew he should pick up.

He stepped out of the conference room to get the news—his mom had just passed away. He knew he didn't have much time to grieve even though he was a mess. He took some time to collect his thoughts and get his head straight before he went back into the conference room.

When he came back to the negotiating table after hearing the news, his demeanor changed. He was visibly upset, his eyes were teary, and he was emotional about the passing of his mom.

James told everyone in the room what happened and the attorneys on the other side of the deal offered to take a few days off and get back together later to finish negotiations. James said he was okay to move forward. At that moment he felt very vulnerable. James was sitting in a room with people who wanted to rip his head off, sharks who smelled blood and could now see that James was wounded. Usually when sharks smell blood they attack.

But something remarkable happened, the sharks didn't attack; they did the opposite. In that moment the impenetrable shields of all of the attorneys and negotiators disappeared and for the next 15 minutes everyone started sharing stories, lessons, and memories of their parents. It showed humanity and that there is more to life than negotiating a business deal. The room was filled with sympathy, empathy, and vulnerability.

James said,

It was interesting because it honestly helped us move past a couple of points that we were all stuck on. They weren't necessarily deal breakers but when negotiating for billions of dollars with some of the world's top attorneys and business leaders, everybody was wanting to win on every single point. This situation caused both sides to say, "You know what, let's move past this, there are bigger things in life than just a business deal." Things went much more smoothly and less aggressively after that.

I had an interesting call after that from the principal at the private equity firm. He said the fact that I allowed others to give me their empathy and sympathy, and that I was accepting of that and embraced it helped create a high level of trust. A lot of deals and negotiations don't actually have high levels of trust, which is why they fall apart. This happened over seven years ago and it proved to be a great deal for both sides and it taught me that being vulnerable can be powerful.

Being able to accept sympathy and empathy is an act of vulnerability, especially for a leader. James could have hidden his feelings and emotions, he could have been a rock, but he chose a different option.

Today, James Fish is the CEO of Waste Management and leads more than 50,000 employees. It's time to lead in a new way, a better way, the vulnerable leader way.

5

How Are You Feeling?

Good is not good enough.

Part of being vulnerable means being able to understand and express your own feelings. It also means you would benefit from making an effort to understand other people's emotions and allow other people to express their feelings.

It's important to remember that the context of the book is about leadership and work, which means acknowledging that leaders play a crucial role and they have a job to do. Actions such as performance, professionalism, serving customers, innovation, growth, profit, and stakeholder value are still relevant and important. You can be as vulnerable as you want, but at the end of the day if as a leader you aren't able to do what is expected of you, then you won't be in that role for very long. Leading with vulnerability will benefit you and everyone around you, if you understand how to do it.

Artie Starrs is the CEO of Topgolf, a modern golf entertainment company with more than 25,000 employees. He made this distinction of leadership very clear to me when we spoke: "One of the best pieces of advice I ever got was from David Gibbs, the current CEO of Yum! Brands. I was talking to him about leaders I admired and he said, 'Every single person you admire has massive insecurities and has made huge mistakes.'

I never thought about that until it really hit me between the eyes! I then looked at all of these leaders with a new lens and thought 'I can do this, too.' Everyone puts their pants on one leg at a time. For me, vulnerability is about closing distance and space between people."

As a leader it's easy to forget that it isn't about you, it's about your people. When it comes to vulnerability it's important to make sure it doesn't become self-indulgent. Ultimately, there needs to be some kind of a business purpose for the vulnerability. It can be about fostering better leaders or creating trust but there needs to be something that can help move your team and your organization forward. If you're just spilling your guts out to everyone and making it all about you, then it doesn't accomplish that forward movement and can in fact prevent progress or growth.

After I had my panic attack, I decided to schedule some sessions with a therapist to see what was going on. One of the exercises she had me do was to check in with myself three times a day to write down how I'm feeling. After doing this for several weeks I realized something very important. I didn't know how to talk about and express how I'm feeling.

I read through several weeks of check-ins and most of the time I would write stuff like "feeling good today" or "feeling a little stressed." But "good" isn't a feeling or an emotion and it doesn't really mean anything; similarly "stressed" can be used as a catch-all for any negative feeling. My therapist then recommended that I look at something called the "feelings wheel," developed by Dr. Gloria Willcox, which is a visual design tool (basically a giant circle of feelings) to help people recognize, talk about, and change their feelings. As I explored the "feelings wheel" I was amazed by all the different ways I could talk about how I was feeling. These weren't new words, but they were words I never used or associated with a feeling or emotion.

Instead of feeling "good," I was able to say I was feeling proud, accepted, powerful, or peaceful. Instead of just saying I was feeling "stressed" or "angry," I was able to say I was feeling critical, disrespected, or let down.

Part of the challenge of being vulnerable isn't just being courageous or bold when it comes to emotional exposure, it's also understanding how to talk about emotions to begin with. What I've learned from thousands of leaders around the world is that this is something most of us struggle with, yet it's something your team members want. One of the reasons we aren't vulnerable is because we don't have the tools or the vocabulary to do so.

This could be due to our upbringing, our current environment, or even a conscientious decision to avoid emotions and all things vulnerability related. Because I grew up watching my dad, vulnerability wasn't a part of my upbringing.

Andy Penn is the CEO of Telstra, an Australian telecommunications company with 50,000 team members. When we spoke, he specifically called out the importance of being able to identify emotions, especially as a leader.

> My mother passed away not that long ago. She was a ferociously independent person, and reflecting on my upbringing now makes me realize I inherited some of those traits. My mother was a nurse her whole life, and she was a busy person who mostly worked nights and supported many seriously ill people. This meant that sometimes my ailments and needs were minor in the scheme of things and I did not feel I could reach out for more emotional support. I learned how to pick myself up if I ever got hurt and get on with life. I learned how to be very self-reliant and not depend on other people for emotional support. But this is actually one of my big personal and professional development initiatives. As a leader you always need to be able to separate the emotion from the issue. This means being able to actually name the emotion that you or someone else is feeling and acknowledging it. Are you feeling anxious? Powerful? Frustrated? Accomplished? Once I am able to identify, reflect, and communicate the emotion that I or someone else on my team is feeling, we're able to get

through and it makes everyone feel much better. It's a bit like being an emotional detective. I still struggle with showing emotion, even with family, but it's something I'm working on and having the ability to identify emotions is a really powerful tool.

Speaking with Andy really reminded me of my family but with the roles reversed. I love my dad very much but he is not comfortable being emotional or vulnerable. My mom, however, is. At a recent dinner at my parents' house, the conversation of favorite books came up. My mom mentioned books including *The Last Kabbalist of Lisbon* and *The Master and Margarita*. My dad mentioned a book called *How Steel Was Tempered*, which is a novel written in the 1930s in the then–Soviet Union about a character named Pavel Korchagin, who gets injured fighting in the Russian Civil War. The premise of the book is how Pavel heals from his injuries and becomes metaphorically strong as steel. I actually read the book to try to understand why it had such an impact on my dad and his life. I understood that he sees himself as Pavel, someone who went through a lot in life and had to be strong and avoid vulnerability and emotion in order to succeed and survive during extremely difficult times. That's how he raised me—to be strong as steel. It's ironic that steel is what robots are made of. Nobody wants to work or live with a robot.

Similar to Andy, I, too, struggle showing emotion and being vulnerable, even with my wife, Blake. I'm really good at sharing what I think and why I think a certain way but that's not where connection comes from. As my wife frequently reminds me, "You can be right or you can be loving." I'm working on being less right and on being more loving. Inside an organization, your people don't just want to know what you're thinking but how you're feeling and why.

Iain Williamson is the CEO of Old Mutual, an African financial services group with more than 30,000 employees. He went through this exact experience.

I received feedback from my team members that I would be a much more effective leader if people knew how I was feeling about something instead of just what I was thinking about something. It wasn't about having a huge outpouring of emotion but being able to name emotions and be specific about them, for example, saying, "I feel productive," "I feel upset," or "I feel motivated." Years ago when I was a CIO, I sensed that there were problems and issues within my team. I told them I felt uneasy and conflicted because we weren't being open and transparent with each other. There were unspoken challenges and tensions that needed to be resolved, which made me feel frustrated. As soon as I shifted to naming and talking about emotions, all of a sudden, all sorts of things came out and we started having brainstorming and whiteboard sessions and everyone started to talk about how they were feeling. As a leader, being vulnerable and talking about emotions creates connection at a much more personal level. It allows you to move from transactional problem-solving to creating relationships that are founded on trust and a deeper understanding of each other. This results in people being there for each other, it unlocks discretionary effort, and it creates a level of collective responsibility.

Most of us think of vulnerability in terms of sharing something negative but we can also feel vulnerable when things are positive as well. Have you ever tried giving a compliment to someone who just wasn't able to receive it? At a recent family get together, my wife told my dad that she thought he had lost some weight. He looked at her and said, "Why should I lose weight? I always look the same." Instead, he could have said, "Thank you for noticing, Blake, I've been trying to eat healthier."

I follow in my dad's footsteps. If someone compliments me and tells me they loved one of my talks or books, I smile and say "thank you," but I have a hard time showing how meaningful those compliments really are to me (which they are).

The assumption is that vulnerability only happens during times of stress, such as asking for help or admitting to a mistake. However, being able to accept praise, gratitude, and positivity also requires vulnerability.

Jay Bray is the chairman and CEO of Mr. Cooper Group, a home loan service company with about 9,000 employees. I was really touched by his candor and willingness to be vulnerable with me about what he struggles with most, and that is being happy and receiving praise. It's not something that gets talked about that much but it's something quite a few people, leaders especially, struggle with. Here's Jay:

> One of the things that make me feel very vulnerable is celebrating, taking time to actually reflect on success or something positive, and being able to congratulate myself and my team. I've shared this with my people as well. There wasn't a lot of celebrating in my house when I was younger; it was always "you can do better" or "what's next?" There was never a real focus on experiencing success. I've come a long way and I've become a lot better at it, but it's something I keep working on.
>
> I am completely comfortable discussing my mistakes, owning up to them, and having a real conversation about them. I have to almost force myself to say, "Okay, Jay, put things in perspective. There's so much to be grateful and thankful for." But I feel like as the leader of the company, it would be really hard to share that because I would feel like it was viewed as a weakness. When I am with team members, I feel like I have to be on, be happy, and be optimistic. I have to be decisive. But when I get off a call, sometimes I'm exhausted. Or sometimes I go back to a dark place, where I don't feel happy, when I don't feel great, and I feel insecure.

I know exactly how Jay feels and this is a huge area of vulnerability that never gets talked about. Leaders are all under tremendous pressure and scrutiny 24/7 and it's not sustainable for any human being.

Letting people in and showing them you have been affected by their words or actions, whether those are negative or positive, requires being vulnerable. Sometimes this requires a change in perspective or having someone help us realize that our recognition of praise can affect others.

Marianne Harrison is the CEO of life insurance company John Hancock, which has about 6,000 employees. Here's what she told me:

> I think our own thoughts can be limiting and keep us from being vulnerable. Imposter syndrome is often held up as an example, but I'm also thinking along the lines of our assumptions that have yet to be challenged. For instance, I wasn't comfortable being called the "first" female CEO of John Hancock. In fact, I didn't realize that was even the case when I took the job. I simply wanted my accomplishments to stand on their own merit. So, that label was not something I chose to embrace. But the feedback that I soon received from younger women about what it meant to see me leading the company as an ally for women at work really opened my eyes. It made me more comfortable with external recognition after seeing how much it could inspire others.

Being able to identify and talk about emotions and feelings whether they are positive or negative is a new and powerful skill for leaders and it's at the heart of becoming a vulnerable leader. This is what enables you to begin climbing the vulnerability mountain.

6

The Land of the Goods

"Hey, how are you?

"Good, and you?"

"Good."

"Okay, see you later."

Have you ever had a conversation like this with a coworker? There is nothing actually being said during this brief exchange, so what's the point? Really what we're saying here is "hi" and getting a "hi" back. You don't get the feeling that the other person is actually interested in how you are doing nor are you honest with the other person about how you are doing. Even though we ask "How are you?" as a greeting we don't expect anyone to answer any other way than "fine" or "good" and most of the time, we aren't really looking for a truthful response.

Most of us work in "the land of the goods" where our organization and everyone around us is always doing "good." It's a polite colloquialism that is used for everything and anything. We know that everyone isn't good. We know that people are feeling proud, stressed, burned out, accomplished, depressed, excited, disrespected, hurt, or optimistic, but we never say that.

John Williams is the CEO of Domtar, which is a 6,500-person paper, pulp, and packaging products company. Here's what he shared with me: "You should not be afraid of letting people know what upsets you or makes you happy, especially if you're a leader. In today's world a lot of leaders especially silence themselves to their real feelings. This is ironic because what makes a great leader is their ability to build relationships, which you cannot do without talking about how you're feeling. Internalizing everything all the time is a toxic way to lead so we need to externalize them in a safe place which will allow those around us to do the same and then we get mutual growth and development."

Instead of asking people "How are you doing?" an effective way to get to some of the deeper feelings and emotions is to change the conversation; the next time you see one of your peers or friends, try asking them one of the following questions:

- What are you working on?
- What are you being challenged with at work today?
- Did you have any wins or successes this week?
- Did you learn anything interesting today?
- Is there a global trend you are paying attention to?
- Are there any ideas you've been wanting to try out at work?
- How do you like to start your day?
- What do you do to wind down in the evenings?

The point is to move away from anything where the other person could respond with things like "good," "fine," or "okay." To use a school analogy you want to move away from a true/false response to an open-ended response. Leaders have to lead by example here.

Therapists use a technique called *I-statements* when working with couples. The premise is that instead of telling your partner "you did ... " or "you made me feel" you replace that with *I*. I feel frustrated, I feel sad, I feel ... you get the idea. As you saw in the example with Iain in Chapter 5, try starting some of your sentences with "I feel."

I-statements force you to acknowledge how you are feeling and help create that connection with those around you as opposed to using you-statements, which can generally be seen as blame and criticism and can act as distance creators.

Consider the following examples of how leaders typically talk and how they can make some slight tweaks to focus on how they are feeling to connect with their people by using I-statements.

"We're going to be screwed if we don't get this project completed."

Instead: "I feel stressed and anxious because we are under a tight deadline and I'm not sure we are going to meet it."

"We closed a new deal today so congratulations to the team."

Instead: "I feel proud of how we came together to close a new deal today; congratulations team."

"I can't believe you didn't promote me. I did everything to get that job and you gave it to someone else."

Instead: "I feel disrespected and let down because I was under the impression that I would get promoted and I worked hard to earn it."

"We are doing a great job and it's making a positive impact."

Instead: "I feel inspired by the work we are doing because it's making a positive impact."

"You made me look stupid in that meeting."

Instead: "I feel embarrassed and disappointed by how you treated me in that meeting."

These very slight adjustments by adding the words "I feel" will enable those around you to connect with you and your message more clearly. These are the statements of a vulnerable leader because you are exposing yourself to the potential of emotional harm while taking action (when possible) to create a positive outcome. We don't connect with our brains; we connect with our hearts.

One of the things my wife and I started doing that has been really helpful is talking about how we're feeling each night before we go to bed. Usually we would lay in bed and watch TV but instead that practice has shifted to us asking, "How are you feeling?" When one of us says "good" the other immediately replies, "That's not an emotion," and it forces us to dig deeper to really reflect on how we are feeling. It creates more connection between us, it enables us to support one another, and it constantly reinforces our trust and love in each other.

Being able to talk about emotions at work should be encouraged, not discouraged. How can we lead with vulnerability and create trust if we don't feel comfortable talking about how we are feeling? Again, it doesn't mean you should turn your workday into a giant therapy session or neglect your responsibilities, but it also doesn't mean you should be a robot. There's a healthy balance. This is not something you can force, but you can work toward it.

Paul Markovich is the CEO of Blue Shield California, a health insurance company with almost 8,000 employees. At the end of 2021 Paul and his company were under enormous pressure and stress with the pandemic. Paul was working 100-hour weeks and it was a very intense period which took a personal toll on Paul.

I was burned out, I couldn't do any more physically, mentally, or emotionally and this also led to high levels of stress in my family as well. I would go through long stretches where I would barely sleep and I had no more resilience left in my body. I would cry almost every day, even knocking over a glass of milk would feel emotionally devastating. I couldn't keep things together and I lashed out at my team when things weren't going the way I wanted them to go. At one point it felt like an out-of-body experience and I couldn't control how I was acting even though I knew I didn't want to act that way. One of my direct reports called me to talk about what's been going on and I just started apologizing to him for the way I behaved. He started giving me feedback about how I made him feel and how my behavior was not acceptable and I just lost it. I started crying on the phone and couldn't stop. He gave me the space to talk about what's going on with me and I told him I need to do better. Sharing personal things like that, I haven't felt that vulnerable in a very long time.

You can imagine how differently this scenario would have played out if Paul's coworker said, "You're the CEO and you're crying? Give me a break and be a man!"

I grew up with that kind of mentality and that response would have actually sounded normal to me but not to most people in the world. This is why it's important to pay attention to cultural differences. For example, as mentioned, in the United States it's very common when greeting someone to just say "How are you doing?" and have the other person respond with "Good, and you?" Then the first person just responds with "Good." In Europe, however, if you ask someone how they are doing, you're likely going to need to sit down with a coffee and get ready to have a longer discussion. Not every culture embraces vulnerability the same way. For some, making a mistake and talking about it can feel shameful and for others it can feel more natural. Having sensitivity to different cultures and geographic locations is important to keep in mind. However, cultural differences doesn't mean that people shouldn't be treated with the same level of respect regardless of where they are.

Blanca Trevino is the president and CEO of Softtek, the leading information technology services company in Latin America with more than 15,000 employees. Blanca is very attuned to cultural differences across various parts of the world but she also expects consistency with how employees are treated.

Years ago we acquired a company in a very different part of the world. I was visiting the company to make the announcement and after I was walking back from a team lunch I saw a group of employees being yelled at by the owner of the company we just acquired. I didn't speak the language so I had no idea what he was saying, but I didn't need to. It was clear to me and everyone else that these employees were not being treated with respect. I interrupted his yelling and said, "I don't know what you're saying but I don't like it and this is not how we treat our people." He looked at me and said, "Blanca, if you don't understand that this is how you must treat people here, then you are going to lose all of your money in this acquisition." I said that I would rather lose my money than lose my culture. I then told the manager who was yelling that the logo on the wall now said Softtek and at Softtek we don't yell and berate people, we treat them with respect. His last words to me were that I would greatly regret treating my people well. Now, a decade later, our business is doing quite well there. When you work at Softtek you are treated with the same level of respect and openness whether you are in Mexico, the US, Argentina, or anywhere else.

Something I learned about myself and leaders when interviewing them is that it is always easy to default to non-vulnerable emotions when we want to express how we feel. For example, let's say you share something private with a coworker who then shares that information with someone else. It's much easier to say you feel angry or furious but these emotions aren't vulnerable, they are more aggressive. If you unpack this a bit further and go one level deeper, the vulnerable emotions are likely things like embarrassment, humiliation, and being disrespected. In other words, part of learning to be vulnerable is sharing and expressing those vulnerable emotions yourself when appropriate.

If you want to lead with vulnerability, there is no hiding from how you feel.

7

Thick Skin but Not Armor

There's an assumption that armoring up means not showing emotion, but that's not entirely true. Armoring up also means avoiding situations and circumstances that would require you to show any emotion or be human to begin with. Some leaders do this by shutting down difficult conversations, avoiding certain topics, or using their power and authority to get others to bend to their will without questioning authority. Bad leaders never take the hits because they don't even put on the uniform to join their team on the field. Great leaders take the hits for their people and keep charging everyone toward the end zone. That's what having thick skin is all about.

Penny Pennington, whom we heard from in Chapter 2, used to wear armor all the time but armor is heavy and uncomfortable and if you wear it long enough, it will exhaust and drain you, which is what happened to Penny: "I have at different points in my life felt that armoring up and putting up a façade of strength and invulnerability and knowing all the answers was the right thing to do. Upon reflection and living that way, what I found was that I wasn't as happy. It takes a lot of energy to armor up. You also don't release yourself fully to creativity and to joy and to being a part of a learning journey. As a leader, when you armor up, you also send a signal to everyone around you that they ought to armor up, too."

If you and everyone around you is walking around with armor on, then how can you possibly be nimble and agile? How will you be able to adapt and lead through change when you don't feel safe to remove the armor and when it's firmly holding you down so you can't move?

There's never been a harder time to be a leader. Your words and decisions are constantly scrutinized and things you say and do can easily get taken out of context. Meanwhile your employees and the communities you serve want you to take a stance on difficult issues and they expect you to . . . well . . . lead!

There's a great scene in the show *Boardwalk Empire* when Steve Buscemi's character Nucky Thompson is talking to Bobby Cannavale's character Gyp Rosetti. Nucky says, "I learned a long time ago not to take things personally." To which Gyp responds, "Everyone's a person, though, right? So how else could they take it?"

Thick skin means you are willing and able to participate in tough conversations, you can handle feedback and even criticism and focus on what can be learned, and you're on the field with your people. It also means you have the capacity to truly listen to what people are telling you. Armor, however, means you are constantly walking around like a bullet-proof tank where you command and control and shut down difficult conversations. Thick skin lets you lead through change; armor confines you to the sidelines as transformation unfolds. As you ascend the vulnerability mountain you will fall and get bruised and banged up. Having thick skin protects you from getting seriously hurt but having armor weighs you down and doesn't allow you to even begin the journey.

When the CEO (who asked to remain anonymous) of a wellness franchise with more than 30,000 employees first got into her role, there was a lot of tension between corporate and the franchisees who were not happy with various decisions being made. She needed to have candid and open conversations with her team members. She understood she needed to have thick skin but that if she went into these discussions with armor on, the relationships would just strain even further.

> I needed to have really thick skin because these conversations got really personal. There were times through finding our way to a better relationship where the trust wasn't there yet, we hadn't found our way far enough, and things got pretty heated and pretty personal. I couldn't get angry, defensive, and shut down. I needed to show up, be present, and listen with an open mind and thick skin. I showed up to the conversations with optimism, positivity, and a vision for the future. Had I put armor on instead of thick skin, I would have put up a huge barrier between myself and the franchisees, which would have really hurt the business. It's been a couple of really challenging years, but we are building trust and really making progress, which comes from the right words followed by the right actions.

The past few years have been hard on all of us. We lost friends and family members during the pandemic. We are struggling to find our way in a turbulent economic and geopolitical landscape. We are faced with polarization that we have never experienced before. For several years many of us have lost the feeling of community, purpose and meaning, and connection as we have worked in a purely virtual world. And we have experienced tragic social injustices and wars. All of these things happened at once, which showed us the importance of having tough conversations at work and being there for each other—being human and vulnerable.

Leaders need to have thick skin, but it's time to lose the armor.

8

How People Become Vulnerable Leaders

Steve Rendle is the chairman, president, and CEO of VF Corporation, which is the parent company behind such iconic brands as Vans, The North Face, Timberland, Dickies, and Jansport. Steve shared a story with me about one of the first jobs he had, in 1983. He was hired by a tough East Coast business leader who was actually fond of Steve because he played lacrosse, which for the CEO denoted toughness. This CEO had no emotion whatsoever, he had all of the answers (or at least pretended he did), and when he asked you to do something you did it. If someone on the team wasn't getting results, there was no coaching or mentoring; the attitude was "if you didn't get the results, then go get them."

One of Steve's first encounters with him during his training was something that belongs in the show *The Office*.

> I'll never forget this. Inside his office he had a desk with a very high chair and on the other side of the desk was a very low couch. When you came in and sat down to speak with him, he was towering over you, showing that he was superior to you. I'd never had this kind of an experience before. I sat down on the couch and it was incredibly uncomfortable so I stood up and spoke to him that way. He just stared at me oddly. I think

he enjoyed and respected that I didn't take part in his game. We worked together for a while and eventually I was able to get past those nuances and see the leader for who he was. In his own way, he did care, but too much of the other stuff got in the way. Leaders don't need to play games, hide that they care, or be scared of being vulnerable. I can only imagine how much more he would have been able to accomplish if he led with vulnerability.

When Steve first told me this story I thought he was joking. Unfortunately, these types of stories or experiences are still common in the business world. I'm always fascinated by them because my question is always "Why?" Why do this to your people? Why treat them like this? I just can't for the life of me understand the goal of this approach. Not only do these types of leaders not climb the vulnerability mountain, they aren't even aware the mountain exists even though it's right in front of them.

How does someone become a vulnerable leader? Unfortunately, some never do but for those who do evolve, or change, where does that evolution come from?

I found that there are three paths leaders take. Either they experience something that transforms who they are, they are taught to be vulnerable leaders by working with a coach, getting employee feedback or teaching themselves, or they were just raised that way.

Although the details of their paths vary greatly, the paths themselves are the same. As you read through these stories, identify which one is most relevant to you and think through that experience and story.

Experience

At some point, life will make you vulnerable. For some leaders it takes a certain event or experience to transform who they are and how they lead. For me, it was having a panic attack, and while I'm still working on being more vulnerable, it was a huge wake-up call that showed me how I'm living and working in this world needs to change.

Jeffrey Katz was the founding CEO of Orbitz Worldwide and former CEO of Swissair. He used to be the stereotypical leader you hear and read about. He practiced a command-and-control style of leadership and he didn't talk about mistakes, failures, or personal struggles. He wore a suit and tie to work, exuded confidence and knowledge, and seemed to have all the answers. He was not a vulnerable leader. One night at about 3 a.m. Jeff got a call that no airline CEO ever wants to get: Swissair Flight 111 had disappeared from the radar. His heart sank. He showed up to the office shortly after and learned that all 229 passengers and crew on that flight had died in a crash—he was never the same leader again.

He saw the emotion and the care that employees had for each other and their customers; Jeff cried with them and grieved with them. He saw the power and the need for compassion and vulnerability and how people come together to support one another during tough times. As Jeff told me, in those types of circumstances there's no room or purpose for the stereotypical bullshit of leadership. This was a pivotal moment for Jeff.

After this experience Jeff told me he became compassionate and emotionally engaged with his people and he gave up his traditional command-and-control style. Today Jeff prioritizes vulnerability. He talks about his challenges and his struggles, and his passions and fears. Jeff communicates with his people openly and focuses on knowing them as human beings and not just workers. This powerful experience transformed Jeff to becoming the vulnerable leader he is today.

The experience doesn't have to be a tragedy and it doesn't have to be something so large in scale. It could be something as small as feedback you received from a team member or leader that flipped a switch. Experience can be a powerful driver for change and for becoming a vulnerable leader but you have to let the experience sink in and absorb it.

Taught

Peter Quigley is the CEO of Kelly Services, a professional services firm with more than 7,000 employees. He was taught to lead with vulnerability.

> When I was six years old, my father abandoned my mother with four young children. She had never worked outside the home and had a lot of responsibility and more debt than money. As you can imagine, we found ourselves in an intense period of financial stress. My mother had to sell our family home and rent an older, smaller house on the other side of town. We borrowed money from friends and family to put food on the table until my mother was able to cobble together part-time work and gain skills and experience to make her way to steady work. My mother showed me—by example—the transformative power of work on people both personally and professionally. Her employment brought our family opportunity and hope. And it certainly changed the trajectory of her life, and consequently mine. I'm fortunate for that, and it's why I do what I do.
>
> From my difficult childhood experiences, I developed some protective behaviors. Early in my career, I felt the need to have two distinct personas: the work Peter and the home Peter. When I showed up to work each day, I wanted to leave the vulnerable Peter who had a tough childhood in the parking lot. I felt pressure to act like the leader with all the answers that I thought I was supposed to be. Becoming a vulnerable leader was a natural evolution for me as I matured as a person and a leader. Even when I stepped into a CEO role, I felt pressure to act "CEO-like," until a coach reminded me that I was named CEO because of who I really am, so I should just be myself. I unlearned the protective defenses I had acquired during childhood and learned the power of just being me.

Today, everyone at the company knows my personal story and they appreciate me for who I am. By leading with vulnerability, people better understand the deep passion I have for the company's purpose of connecting people to work in ways that enrich their lives.

I was fascinated to hear how many of the CEOs I interviewed or worked with have teamed up with a coach. This alone can be viewed as an act of vulnerability, and even five years ago admitting to working with a coach would have been taboo.

We forget how different the business world was over the past few decades. Most leaders around the world went to schools and worked in organizations where concepts like vulnerability, emotional intelligence, decentralized decision-making, employee experience, and stakeholder (not shareholder) value were never taught, and in fact were actually discouraged!

It's important for us to remember this because I genuinely don't believe that most leaders are bad people. I don't believe that leaders are all sitting in their corner offices thinking of how they can make our lives miserable. This is an evolution for all of us and leaders around the world are having to unlearn and relearn what it means to lead. We need to guide, help, and support each other.

How You Were Raised

How you are raised plays a profound role in shaping who you are as a person and as a leader. I shared some of my family history previously, which profoundly shaped me. Some leaders were raised embracing and practicing being vulnerable and they carry that with them through their careers and into their leadership roles.

One such leader is Sal A. Abbate, the CEO of Veritiv, a 6,000-person company that provides packaging, janitorial and sanitation, and hygiene products, services, and solutions.

Here's what he shared with me during our interview:

Who you are and where you come from shapes a lot about where you go. I grew up in a small town in Poughkeepsie, New York, which has about 35,000 people. I come from a very traditional Italian family. All four of my grandparents were immigrants from Italy, and my parents are first-generation Americans. They grew up in the Italian section of New York, which was Manhattan and Queens.

I'm the youngest of five and I have four older sisters. We are a very tight-knit family. I was raised where showing emotion and being vulnerable wasn't just okay but encouraged. I talk about my family and share my stories and experiences. In my household, dinner was a big event, not just once a month but every night, and certainly on weekends. That's where everybody gathered to share their grievances. In fact, our friends, who were not from the same Italian heritage, would come over for dinner just for the theater. We had big personalities, from my mother and my grandfather, and they were particularly critical, but not mean. So early on I learned how to take feedback and how to improve. It wasn't organized, it was kind of chaotic, but it was fun. At the end of the day, we hugged, we cried, we laughed, and we kissed. There were zero grudges. Everybody knew where everybody stood.

I remember a time when a CEO actually tried to coach me and told me never to apologize, say I don't know something, or show emotion. I thought this was a terrible way to lead and it went against how I was raised so I never did that.

I grew up a vulnerable leader and that's how I will continue to be and teach others to be.

Over the course of the interviews I conducted, a few CEOs shared how their families and their past have had a profound impact on shaping who they are as a person and as a leader today.

Regardless of how these leaders become vulnerable leaders, the important thing is that they each followed a path that helped them become who they are. I was raised in a way where I didn't believe in or accept vulnerability. Over the years I have become more comfortable with vulnerability, but my panic attacks were an experience that profoundly changed my perspective.

In a follow-up survey that DDI and I conducted with 1,200 people, we asked which one of the three paths to vulnerable leadership they credit for being a vulnerable leader (they were able to select more than one answer). Experience came in at 76%, being taught came in at 37%, and being raised in a way that encouraged vulnerability came in at 20%.

Some leaders have never experienced something that transformed them to lead with vulnerability, were not taught to be vulnerable leaders, or were not raised in an environment that encouraged vulnerability. If they have, they consciously and purposefully avoid vulnerability because they are stuck in an anti-vulnerability loop that needs to be broken.

If you consider these three paths, you will realize that you have already been on at least one of them.

II

What Prevents Leaders from Being Vulnerable at Work?

9

Why Don't We Have More Superheroes?

I f a vulnerable leader is this amazing superhero who can positively affect the lives of those around them, then why don't we have more superheroes at work (see Figure 9.1)? Specifically, survey respondents were asked, "What prevents you from being vulnerable at work?"

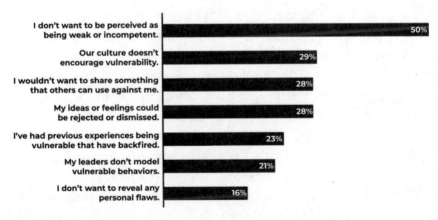

Figure 9.1 Percentage of high-quality leaders in organizations

The number-one thing by far across the board that prevents leaders from being vulnerable at work is that they don't want to be perceived as weak or incompetent. This was also true across every single industry that was surveyed. This is why vulnerability plus competence can be a powerful combination, and vulnerability without competence can prove to be disastrous, something that will be explored in Chapter 22.

In second place is a lack of culture that supports vulnerability, followed by the fact that ideas or feelings could be rejected or dismissed. Although having ideas or feelings being rejected or dismissed is tied for third on the list, when slicing the data across levels, its priority decreases with seniority. Meaning, the more senior you become, the less concerned you are with having your ideas or feelings be dismissed by others. This makes sense because typically the more senior you are the more decision-making power, authority, and credibility you have.

Sharon Price John is the president and CEO of Build-A-Bear Workshop, which has about 3,000 employees. We talked about this breakdown and she shared a valuable perspective:

> By definition, taking on a broadened leadership role that includes new functional areas reporting into you means that you will be put into a position where you don't know how to do something and/or don't have experience doing it. In that respect, the more senior you become, the more you "don't know" because your responsibilities will eventually expand beyond your expertise. When I became the CEO of my company, I had not run IT, a warehouse, sourcing, HR, or operations, yet those areas were reporting to me. By leading with vulnerability, I could surround myself with people who had knowledge in these areas to help me. While it may be uncomfortable for some that they would be put in a position with a reporting structure stretched beyond their core competencies with people reporting to them who have skills

and expertise beyond their own, this is a necessary step to obtain certain roles, particularly a CEO role. And, showing enough vulnerability to learn from others would have likely already been mastered, or they would not have advanced to that level at all.

The common thread behind all of the responses is that they challenge the conventional idea and stereotype of who a leader is. Leadership is not about what you know but about what you can unlock in those around you (and in yourself).

10

Breaking the Leadership Stereotype

It was a dark and stormy night, a ship captain was sitting writing in his log when all of a sudden one of his officers ran in.

"Captain, we have a huge problem! There's a ship 10 miles ahead of us and it refuses to get out of the way!"

The captain looks up and says, "Don't they know who we are? Tell them to move!"

"We tried that sir, they refused."

The captain gets up from his chair, puts on his hat and jack and says, "Well, then I'll tell them myself."

He walks over to the bridge and sends out a message, "Move starboard 15 degrees at once."

A message comes back, "You move starboard 15 degrees at once."

The captain is shocked. Who would dare speak to him in such a way? He gets back on the radio, "This is Captain James. T Smith III and I'm ordering you to move starboard 15 degrees now."

A message comes back, "This is Fred. You move starboard 15 degrees yourself."

At this point the captain is furious and turning red, all of his officers are looking at him wondering what he's going to do next. He sends out one last message, "This is the *U.S.S. Missouri*. We are the largest, the greatest, and most powerful ship in the US naval fleet, and if you do not move starboard 15 degrees now, then I will be forced to take action."

A few seconds go by and a message comes back. "This is the lighthouse. It's your call."

■ ■ ■

Leaders of organizations around the world believe that they are these big battleships who can just pick a destination and using outdated approaches, reach that destination, and achieve success. This is not leading through change; it's leading into stagnation.

This approach to leadership no longer works. It's time for us to shift course or we're all going to crash into the lighthouse. As Marshall Goldsmith famously says, "What got you here, won't get you there!"

Our brains are perhaps the world's greatest storage devices. The memory capacity of the human brain is 2.5 petabytes. This is the equivalent of almost 28,000 4K quality movies or 50 million tall filing cabinets filled with information. How do we make sense of all this information stored in our brains? Two very effective methods are schemas and stereotypes, and entire books and fields of study are devoted to exploring this.

Schemas are mental shortcuts that help guide our behaviors and decisions in situations. For example, a schema will tell you how to act in a fancy restaurant, how to behave at a dinner party, or how to behave in a workplace setting. In each of these situations your brain uses its massive data set to make generalizations about how to act and what you should or shouldn't say.

At work, for example, our schemas are based around actions such as professionalism, confidence, showing dedication and loyalty, not being emotional, and being productive. If you think about your schema for work and for home, you will realize there are very clear differences between the two.

A stereotype, however, is a schema you have for people. Consider the following riddle.

A father and his son are in a terrible car accident. The father dies on impact, but the son gets taken to the hospital for surgery. Once in the operating room, the surgeon takes one look at the boy and says, "I can't operate on him. He's my son."

Who is the surgeon?

His mom!

In a recent paper called "I Can't Operate, That Boy Is My Son!": Gender Schemas and a Classic Riddle," the authors administered this riddle to 152 college students in the United States. Only 30% stated the surgeon could be a woman, whereas 36% of them said the surgeon could be a second father in a same-sex marriage.[1] Think about them for a moment. Our stereotype of a doctor being a male in a white lab coat is so strong that in the riddle we would rather assume the surgeon is a second father than accept that the surgeon could be a woman.

Stereotypes and schemas can be beneficial and detrimental to our success. In the case of vulnerability and leadership, our schemas about the workplace and our stereotypes of leaders go against the notion that vulnerability is accepted and is indeed a powerful trait for leaders to have. The CEO interviews I did prove this.

Pam Maynard is the CEO of Avande, a global professional services firm with almost 60,000 employees globally.

I vividly remember early on in my career that I got on the elevator and a gentleman who was already in there asked me if I was a new secretary. He tried to direct me to the secretarial pool. Immediately I had a feeling of "I don't belong here." That experience taught me early in my career what my mom had always encouraged growing up: use my voice and speak up. So, I did just that. I extended my hand, told him my name was Pam Maynard and I was a consultant. This experience is why, to this day, I encourage women in particular to find their voice—and use it—at every stage of their career. Finding and using your voice is vulnerability made real—and that's not always easy.

When I've had trouble finding my voice, I've asked mentors for advice and support to help me with tactics to create opportunities for me, and to challenge me to share my opinions. That helped me build the confidence I have today and allowed me to grow as a leader. And because of that, it's also something that I'm conscious of helping others with.

Think about all of the different leadership stereotypes we have that today are completely not true, even though some of them were ironically taught to us:[2]

- A leader should never apologize.
- A leader should not show emotion.
- A leader should always be strong and confident.
- A leader always needs to have the right answers.
- A leader needs to take charge.
- A leader needs to be the smartest person in the room.
- A leader should never be questioned.

Toward the end of 2022 I started doing an ongoing series of articles on my LinkedIn page, where I argue in favor of stereotypical leadership. These are satirical posts with titles like:

"Put on Your Big Kid Pants and Come to Work!"

"Why Great Leaders Don't Apologize"

"Nobody Cares About Your Problems at Work!"

"Forget Soft Skills. You Need to Be the Smartest Person in the Room"

"Why Trusting Your Employees Is Bad and Why They Need to Earn It"

"Don't Look Your CEO in the Eyes!"

"Who Should You Promote? The Overworkers"

"Why Listening to Your People Is Overrated"

At the end of each article, I signed off with The Outdated Leader so people would know the posts were meant as satire. Little did I know many people wouldn't read to the very end!

My articles were flooded with comments ranging from people who loved the satire to others who thought I lost my mind. Many of the comments were fierce arguments and criticisms against the views of The Outdated Leader.

The goal of these articles was to get people to challenge stereotypes of leadership and to argue against what I was writing. I was surprised to see that many people who commented wrote that they worked for organizations and leaders where the satire was reality. The Outdated Leader is alive and well in most organizations around the world, including yours.

Do you know anyone who would write or support articles like the ones I wrote? More important, do you want to work with someone like this?

I've yet to meet someone who says, "This Outdated Leader sounds like my dream leader."

Stanley Bergman is the CEO of Henry Schein, a 22,000-person company that distributes health-care products. He shared something simple and profound with me that challenges the stereotype of leaders: "I want people around me who are smarter than me and better than me. A CFO's job is to ensure the company doesn't run out of cash. The CEO's job is to ensure that you don't run out of leadership."

Almost everyone I interviewed told me that early in their careers they were not vulnerable leaders. Vulnerability wasn't taught in MBA programs, and it wasn't encouraged or modeled inside of organizations. These things went against the stereotype of who a leader is and what they should be like. A leader is supposed to always be in control, to be confident and competent, to have all the answers, and not to get emotional. The fascinating thing is that we also interact more with people who share our stereotypes, which in a corporate setting will simply reinforce and strengthen them, in this case, that *vulnerable* and *leader* shouldn't go in the same sentence!

Chris Caldwell is the CEO of Concentrix, a global customer experience services and technology company with more than 300,000 employees. He shared an interesting story with me:

I worked with one individual who believed that as a leader, they were unquestionable, and if they made a decision, they would simply never say they were wrong, because they saw it as weakness. I always thought of it as "if you're driving off a cliff, you'd rather be right, going in the right direction, but then dead at the bottom?" They saw being a vulnerable leader as weakness.

I also worked for someone else whom I have a lot of respect for, a brilliant and smart person who also believed that as a leader you must never be vulnerable because it's a sign of weakness. They believed in never engaging in friendly banter or getting to know anyone on a human level, it was business from eight until six, and that's it. Friends are separate from coworkers. I only saw who this person really was maybe two or three times but it was very quick and then they turned back into a rock.

Both of these people lacked any kind of vulnerability and emotional intelligence and they didn't understand that their behavior drove the business. They would get frustrated with the outcomes and not knowing, then things didn't go well but they couldn't see that it was their lack of vulnerability that drove that. Their mentality was "my way or the highway." I remember giving them feedback one day suggesting that they try a different approach and the response was, "I'm not here for a counseling session and I'm not married to you." I learned a lot from these leaders both in terms of what to do but also what to not do.

The fascinating thing is that these same CEOs, who now lead multibillion-dollar companies, all told me this stereotype of leaders is wrong. That doesn't make sense, right? If CEOs are saying the leadership stereotype is wrong, then why does that stereotype exist to begin with?

When we first get a job we are taught that our primary goal is to focus on a specific task or project, for example, handling customer service requests, working on product design, or trying to fill open positions in a department. However, when we get promoted to a leadership position our primary goal moves from focusing on the task to focusing on the people who are responsible for the tasks. Now all of a sudden we move from "how can I best accomplish this task" to "how can I unlock the potential of my people so they can best accomplish their tasks?" It's at this point that leaders realize the importance of connecting with their people and—you guessed it—being vulnerable.

In other words, the stereotypes and schemas for some leaders are not the same as they are for individual contributors. They get rewritten as the world changes and as their assumptions are challenged. They realize emotion creates connection, confidence needs to be tempered with humility, not having the answers leads to growth and discovery, and vulnerability isn't a weakness that should be eliminated but a superpower that should be unleashed.[3]

It's as if when someone becomes a leader they are taken out of the matrix and put into the real world. This, of course, isn't true for every leader and for every company but almost every CEO I interviewed reflected this.

But what if you could change the schema and the stereotype of work and leadership earlier on in the lives of your employees? What if you could make it so that when employees first start working at your company, their goal is immediately focusing on people and not just the task. Of course, the task is still important, but within the context of people.[4]

Tiger Tyagarajan is the CEO of Genpact, a professional services firm with more than 115,000 employees globally. Being able to challenge this leadership stereotype has been the single greatest factor of his success.

At one of his first jobs in the consumer goods space in India, he was responsible for a team of seven people, all of them older than Tiger. He was intimidated and scared when he took on the role. However, he knew he had a choice to either take on the role of leader by acting in a stereotypical command-and-control style or be vulnerable. On his first day on the job, he went up to an employee whom everyone referred to as the god of the sales team and said, "I don't know anything about this role or sales and I'm going to look to you to teach me and guide me. I want to learn from you." This employee had a reputation for not being very welcoming to new team members but he looked at Tiger and said, "You're going to be like my son in this company. I'm going to teach you everything and if you ever have any problems or questions, you come and talk to me."

As Tiger told me,

Even though I was his boss, that five-minute conversation where I was vulnerable with him completely transformed our relationship and I took that with me into every other role and company I've ever had. Even today if I work with junior employees who have only been at the company for a year, if they tell me they are working on something like artificial intelligence, I tell them that I don't know much in that space and I ask them if they can teach me. The reaction from team members is always "Wow, I'm going to teach the CEO something" and for me, it's another bridge I get to build and something new I get to learn. Had I not been vulnerable early on in my career, I would not have ended up where I am now.

There is one bulletproof way to change the leadership stereotype: lead by example. If as a leader you aren't willing to be vulnerable, then why would anyone on your team want to be vulnerable with you or with each other? You can't command or ask other people to be vulnerable leaders unless you are one yourself.

Constantinos G. V. Coutifaris and Adam Grant recently did some research on how leaders can create psychological safety and build trust by going against the stereotypical leader who always conveys strength, confidence, and knowledge. They discovered that one of the key ways leaders can show vulnerability is by sharing criticisms and suggestions that they have received about their own performance. In Study 1, they found that leaders who share feedback on their own performance created psychological safety among their top management teams. In Study 2, they found that when leaders shared feedback it had a positive impact on team psychological safety one year later. The interesting thing, though, is that simply seeking feedback didn't create that same sense of safety. In Study 3, they found that when leaders initiated vulnerability by seeking feedback, it created short-term positive impact on psychological safety in their teams but that this eventually dissolved. However, leaders who actually shared the feedback they received were able to create long-term psychological safety. Therefore, the advice for leaders isn't to just seek feedback but to actually share the criticisms and the feedback that they receive. When I interviewed Constantinos he told me, "When leaders are forthcoming about their own shortcomings with employees, they offer tangible evidence that they have listened to and can handle criticism. Opening the door to bottom-up feedback can normalize and crystallize vulnerability in teams, which helps build psychological safety over time."

Nancy Brown is the CEO of the American Heart Association. She says this rather eloquently: "The best way to encourage vulnerability in your teams is to demonstrate it yourself. Leaders have to nurture an environment that rejects phrases such as, 'We've always done it that way' and 'That's not my job.'"

Going against the grain is not an easy thing to do, but it's vital. If you want to break the leadership stereotype at your company, then it's going to start with how you show up to work each day and how you interact with those around you.

Figure 10.1 shows a simple framework you can use to challenge and break leadership stereotypes inside of your organization.

| Lead by Example | Empower Others | Adapt | Develop Leaders |

Figure 10.1 How to break leadership stereotypes

Lead by Example

If you break the stereotype, then those around you will know it's okay to do so as well. Leaders have a responsibility to pave the way for others.

Empower

Give those around you the power to challenge convention. Encourage them to come up with new ideas to problems and let them know it's okay if they fail or make a mistake.

Adapt

It's tempting to get back into your comfort zone and cover yourself with the warm blanket of "we've always done it like that here." That's not where growth happens. When you develop new ideas and approaches, make them official.

Develop

In my book, *The Future Leader*, I discovered that although most people become leaders at some point in their 20s they don't actually get official training until they are in their mid- to late

30s or early 40s. That means people spend anywhere from 10 to 20 years leading others without being taught how to do so. Give everyone at your company the opportunity to participate in leadership development and training programs. If you want to break the leadership stereotypes, then teach everyone what it means to lead.

This simple and practical framework will enable you and your team to take a hard look at the leadership stereotypes inside of your organization and how you can change them into something that benefits everyone who works there. You can't lead with vulnerability if you cling to old ways of doing things.

What Makes Leaders Feel Vulnerable?

11

The 10 Vulnerability Signs

Not everyone expresses vulnerability in the same way nor does everyone find the same things to be vulnerable. We can be vulnerable during scary or big moments, such as receiving candid feedback from a trusted peer or when we need to let someone go because of performance issues. We can also be vulnerable every day with small moments, such as praising someone on a team, asking for help, or even listening to someone. Not every act of vulnerability needs to be large in scale and impact. Everyday vulnerability is what enables you to be vulnerable in those big moments when needed.

It's important to understand some of the most common signs or languages of vulnerability for leaders so we can identify them and then respond accordingly. The caveat for all of these is that the leader is genuine. Take asking for help as an example. There are a few ways this can be done. In one scenario, I can say something such as, "I'm really struggling with this project I'm working on and I could really use your help." Or I can say, "Hey, I need you to do something for me because I'm not able to." In both situations, I'm asking for help but you get the sense that in the first scenario I'm being genuine and vulnerable whereas in the second scenario I'm actually trying to create space and avoid vulnerability. How things are said and perceived makes a difference.

The second thing to keep in mind is that for each person some of these things may be more or less vulnerable. For you, asking for help might be a very vulnerable act, whereas for another leader on the team they just view it as a way of getting work done. That's okay; it's still a vulnerability signal to pay attention to. A final point to remember is that a signal doesn't have to mean vulnerability.

Have you ever driven along a windy road and seen a sign that looks like rocks falling on a car? It means to watch out when driving because rocks can fall from the side of a cliff or mountain you are driving near. It doesn't mean rocks are falling on your head at that moment, and in most cases rocks won't fall at all, but it's still a sign you need to pay attention to.

The vulnerability signs are the same. It doesn't necessarily mean that someone is feeling or being vulnerable at that moment but it's a sign they might be, which means they are signs worth paying attention to.

As you go through these, keep in mind the Vulnerable Leader Equation, which was described in detail in Chapter 2:

(V) Vulnerability + (L) Leadership = (VL) Leading with Vulnerability

Recall as well the definition of a vulnerable leader: "a leader who intentionally opens himself or herself up to the potential of emotional harm while taking action (when possible) to create a positive outcome."

Based on the more than 100 CEO interviews I did, these are the 10 most common signs of vulnerability among leaders (see Figure 11.1). Our follow-up survey with DDI from nearly 1,200 participants also asked, "Which one of the following are best examples of how you convey feeling vulnerable to others." Respondents were able to select all relevant choices.

| Asking for help | Listening | Admitting to a mistake | Asking for or receiving candid feedback | Sharing personal information including a challenge or struggle |
| Talking about risk or uncertainty | Giving or receiving praise | Being in a tough situation | Being authentic | Showing sincere emotion |

Figure 11.1   10 signs of vulnerability

Asking for Help

Asking for help can be something small, such as figuring out how to work a piece of technology, or something large, such as getting help with a large client project that is on a tight deadline. Of course, how vulnerable the leader feels will depend on the leader but what I have observed is that the greater the impact of the project or the ask, the more vulnerable the leader will feel. For example, asking for help with the WiFi password is oftentimes not going to make someone feel as vulnerable as asking for help on making a strategic business decision that will affect the lives of team members. It's important to pay attention to the small and big asks for help because they can both signal vulnerability.

Nurtac Afridi is the global CEO of GODIVA, a 3,000-person chocolate-making company. Here's what she told me: "When I joined the company, I admitted to Tara, who is on my team, that I'm not a very strong public communicator and that I would really need her help. So I ask her for help and feedback whenever I'm giving presentations or doing any kind of public communication. I'm still learning and developing but whenever I have to go on a stage or be near a microphone I get very nervous and feel vulnerable so I ask for help. It's something I'm determined to work on and improve with each presentation or public appearance."

Notice the emphasis she makes around turning this into a learning and development moment. It's tempting to assume that if something doesn't make you feel vulnerable, it also won't make someone else vulnerable, but that is rarely the case. This is a common mistake we make, especially at work. When someone asks you for help, it's always important to take a step back and think, "This person might be feeling vulnerable."

Admitting to a Mistake

Admitting a mistake is hard for leaders to do; in fact, nobody enjoys talking about their mistakes or failures and taking accountability for them. Vulnerable leaders are able to turn their mistakes into learning moments, and they accept responsibility for them instead of blaming others. Talking about a mistake or a failure is another sign of vulnerability you need to pay attention to.

My favorite example of this comes from Lard Friese, the CEO and chairman of the executive and management board at Aegon, a Dutch financial services group with more than 22,000 employees:

> I remember having a burning ambition to progress. When I was 35, I learned a very harsh lesson, which was a real turning point for me and forced me to think differently as a leader. At a young age I was made the leader of a very large business unit and I had to introduce a new technology platform in that unit. I was warned by my peers that it wasn't working well and that it shouldn't be implemented but against all the advice I pushed it through. This backfired bigtime.
>
> It led to a complete rejection of the platform but more importantly a complete rejection of me by my team. The people who were working for me in that unit believed I shouldn't be in that job, and I was removed from it. I came home only to find out that my wife was also on the brink of firing me! She told me I wasn't around and that I was neglecting

her and our kids and I wasn't being a good father. You can imagine this was just the perfect storm. This all happened just before Christmas so my family and I took a 10-day vacation and luckily she gave me a second chance, and she's still my wife and we now have a wonderful family life.

When I came back to work I told my leaders I didn't want to be removed from my job and placed elsewhere in the company. Instead I asked to be demoted in that business unit because I wanted to clean up my own mess and to regain the trust of my people whom I once abandoned as a leader. I worked for several years to make amends and at the beginning it was really hard.

I had to admit to my mistakes and to talk about them openly and to reflect deeply on my behaviors. I had to lead with vulnerability and I truly saw the power of that because it allowed me to connect with my team on a different and deeper human level. I earned back that trust that I had lost and it was an absolute pinnacle crucible moment in my career when I truly understood how important it is to be aware and vulnerable.

The first thing I did was to make sure that people understood that I owned the problem. Secondly, they needed to understand what my intentions were. That this wasn't an ego trip, but I was truly and genuinely trying to fix my mistake. It required a lot of listening. I listened not only with my ears, but also with my heart. And the most important thing was them realizing that I was asking for help. I had a realization that the most powerful question I could ask someone was, "Can you please help me?" I didn't just ask with my mouth or brain, but with my heart; it was real.

I wanted to help the company become better. I knew I messed up. I asked the team to give me a chance. When I did that, asking for help was a sign of strength, not weakness. Suddenly people noticed and were ready to help me. I needed to go through that personal experience in order to have that insight. With small steps I earned my way back, and I realized that people see through your actions. They need to know that what you're doing comes from a place that is genuine and authentic, not concocted or made up.

I've worked with and interviewed thousands of CEOs over the years, but I've never heard of a leader like Lard get fired from a position and then ask to return to the team they got fired from with a demotion in order to fix their mistakes. This is the very definition of being a vulnerable leader, taking accountability, admitting to a mistake, learning from the mistake, and then taking the steps needed to fix it.

Sharing Personal Information Including a Challenge or Struggle

Not all leaders are comfortable sharing personal information about themselves or their lives at work. They prefer to have more clearly defined boundaries, which is, of course, a choice we can all make. However, there are also leaders who are more comfortable with letting people into their personal lives when appropriate. One such leader is Tom Polen, the chairman, CEO, and president at BD, one of the largest global medical technology companies with more than 75,000 employees.

One day when I was 13, I was getting ready for school like any other day. My mom was helping us when she suddenly collapsed in convulsions in front of me in our living room. She was rushed to the hospital and admitted immediately into the shock trauma unit. At the end of the day she was pronounced dead, having passed away of a massive brain aneurysm. She was completely healthy, extremely fit, and 35 years old. That experience at an early age was my first real exposure to health care. It was a day I'll never forget as I went through the health care journey by her side, watching the process as it occurred to my mom. From then on, I always had a deep passion and interest in health care and making it better. It inspired me, and continues to inspire me today, to do what we do at BD—to improve patient outcomes, help providers deliver the best care, and ultimately help people live better lives. I share this personal story with my team to help everyone understand why I do what I do, why what we do matters, and the impact that we can have on the world.

Tom touches on an important element, which is sharing personal information with intention. It's not an expectation for leaders to get into the nitty-gritty of their personal lives, but it can be powerful and it's definitely a sign of vulnerability.

I learned this when I left my last corporate job over 15 years ago and started building my own team. At the beginning, I wasn't very open with anyone. I focused purely on tasks and projects and kept anything personal out of the mix. The business did okay, but we had lots of challenges. I noticed we weren't experimenting with new ideas, nobody would come forward to share their challenges or feedback, the work felt routine and monotonous, and we didn't feel connected to each other or the work. It didn't feel like a team.

Today I'm much more comfortable sharing personal information with my team. I talk about my kids and all the weird things they do and say. I shared when I had my panic attack and how terrified I was. I told my team how stressful our move was from San Francisco to Los Angeles. I send pictures of my dogs and sometimes have them make an appearance in our team calls. I even share what my wife and I go out and do during our date nights.

Sharing my personal challenges and experiences outside of work has helped me create a much higher level of trust and connection with my team. We personally and professionally support each other when someone is going through a tough time. We more freely share ideas and feedback. The quality of work has improved, and the work we do has a greater sense of meaning. We feel like a team and the business has grown considerably.

Giving or Receiving Praise

We assume that vulnerability always has to deal with negative emotions, but being able to give and receive praise can be a sign of vulnerability as well because it does require emotional exposure. Showing you're proud, supportive, or grateful is a sign of vulnerability, as is receiving praise from other people.

Jason Randall is the president and CEO of AppFolio, a real estate cloud business management with almost 2,000 employees: "I had told someone that they were doing well in a group setting. It wasn't anything planned. It was just something that I noticed, but it wasn't a platitude; it was genuine. That person came up to me afterward and told me that it meant a lot to him and that the praise was really powerful. That echoed right back into me and I felt the emotion of it, too. We both felt vulnerable and it was all from a positive experience."

Did you notice anything particular about what Jason said? The most important word in that entire quote is *genuine*, meaning he believed and meant what he was saying. Previously I've mentioned that people can tell when you are faking it and that can lead to the erosion of trust, missed opportunities for learning and growth, and a toxic workplace culture.

Being in a Tough Situation

Being aware of other people's situation is an important and powerful skill to have, especially when it comes to being a vulnerable leader. All of the other signs discussed in this section are observable signs. However, there are also times when someone is put in a tough situation. For example, let's say you are tasked with taking over a project or a team that has previously seen poor success. Think of Lard's situation from earlier: even if he didn't say a single word, it's important to identify that the situation he was in would make him and most people feel vulnerable.

Garry Ridge is the former CEO of WD-40 Company, and he shared a story with me of how he reacted when he noticed that one of his team members was in a tough spot. Without getting into confidential details Garry told me that this individual was having a very bad morning and wasn't creating a positive lasting memory, something Garry and his team strive for, as it is a stated value of the company.

At the end of the meeting I offered that tribe member to take a walk. As we got outside I started looking around as if I was looking for something. I have to admit it may have seemed like I was acting strangely. I was looking under a car, behind trash cans and trees. At some point this person asked what the hell I was doing. And my response was "I'm looking for you. The person I know and love was not in that room today. You create positive lasting memories all the time but not today. What's on your mind and how can I help you?" We had a meaningful conversation and then we went back into the office and I saw them going to a couple of people who were in that meeting and apologizing. People reacting in embraces even, admitting that they knew something was off, and asking what was going on and how they could make that person's day better. Having a set of values that allows you to bring out vulnerability and transparency further allows you to act on a situation that if we didn't that toxic kind of fumes would have continued, and that person would have continued to have a bad day.

When you notice someone around you in a tough spot, they are almost always feeling vulnerable. Respond with kindness, compassion, and a willingness to help if you can.

Listening

Hearing is the unconscious act of letting sound enter your ear but listening requires purpose, attention, focus, and commitment. It requires that you pay attention to body language, remove distractions, ask relevant questions, and make the other person feel seen and heard. You move the attention away from yourself and onto someone else. This is a sign of vulnerability.

Jerry Norcia is the CEO of DTE Energy, a Detroit-based energy company with about 10,000 employees. He understands that listening is a powerful vulnerability sign:

> Being an engineer, my instinct is to always try to help people solve whatever they are up against. As I grew as a leader, I realized that sometimes people just want you to listen and not have the answer or to come up with the solutions or action plans . . . just listen. This is a hard and vulnerable thing to do. Specifically in moments of crisis, I have become much better at listening, which is difficult for a hands-on leader like me. By listening and being a vulnerable leader, I'm able to learn about people's life stories, where they come from, what they need help with and what ideas they might have to improve or solve a problem.

We've all been in a situation in which someone comes to us with a problem and we are very quick to come up with a solution we know is going to work. We present our miraculous idea only to find that it doesn't land well. How come? If only they would listen to us, all of their problems would be solved and they would be so much happier!

The problem is that the other person isn't always looking for advice or a solution; they just want you to listen and acknowledge what they are saying and how they are feeling. I struggle with this all of the time, and it's something I try to work on. I always feel like I have great ideas about anything and everything, but one of the most important things I've learned is that the best thing I can do is to shut up and listen unless someone specifically asks me for advice. For me, Jerry, and many other leaders out there, being able to just be present and listen is a tough and vulnerable thing to do.

Asking for or Receiving Candid Feedback

Giving and receiving feedback is easy. Giving and receiving candid feedback can be brutal. We've all experienced both of these things. How many times have you asked someone for feedback only to get broad, general, sugarcoated responses that you can't really do anything with? How many times have you received feedback from someone that was hard to hear but actually helped you grow and develop? That's the feedback that really matters.

Chris Toth is the CEO of Varian, a Siemens Healthineers company with more than 11,000 employees. Here's what he shared with me:

> I was 30 years old and just took over the global marketing team. I had individuals reporting to me who were longer tenured, more experienced, intelligent, strategic, and had valuable and diverse perspectives. I came into the role with extreme pressure in myself and the insecurity of being young in such a senior role. I felt like I needed to prove myself and what I failed to understand was that the definition of proving myself wasn't coming and saying, "Here are all the changes we need to make and how're we're going to do them." It should have been listening first and then learning passionately, which are two of the values we have today. Instead I came in and I drove hard. I talked about how we needed to change the way we work and the problems I wanted to solve. Luckily I had some members of the team give me some honest feedback. They told me, "Hey, you're losing the team by just driving so hard in your direction, and you have to stop. We can't work with you like this." At that moment I stopped, acknowledged what the team was saying, and apologized. I changed the conversation from focusing on me to focusing on the team—what we need to address, the deficiencies we have as a team, and the problems we should solve. Sometimes leaders either knowingly or

unknowingly can push too hard and try to force their will. It doesn't mean it comes from a bad place. The only way to discover these things is by getting candid feedback, which is a very vulnerable yet necessary thing to do, especially for leaders.

Leaders are especially challenged in this area because not only should they get candid feedback from their peers but also from anyone and everyone on the team who is willing to give it to them to help them improve. I have a team of 12 people. I want candid feedback from every single one of them about where I can improve and how I can make their lives and their job easier.

Talking About Risk or Uncertainty

It feels like with each passing year, we are faced with more change and uncertainty. In most business environments leaders don't acknowledge or talk about that uncertainty because it goes against the stereotype of who a leader needs to be. Being able to say, "I don't know what the answer is" or "I'm not sure what direction to take" is a very clear sign of vulnerability.

Scott Gutz is the CEO of Monster Worldwide, a 2,000-person company that connects people and jobs.

When I joined the company it was a turnaround situation and the business was in a really tough spot. I had to have open and honest conversations with people about risk and uncertainty that were tough, including things I saw in the business that weren't working well, poor decisions that were being made, and competitors that were moving quickly in areas we weren't investing in. It's okay to have these conversations but it's not okay as a leader to just say that everything is broken and that it's someone else's fault. I told everyone that we were going to work together to chart a course that allows Monster to change and move in a different direction. One of the first messages I delivered to the team in my first week as CEO was "I don't know exactly how we are going to change and right the ship but I will tell you that within the first 6 to 12 months we are going to come together and figure out areas where we can focus on growth and opportunity." I was vulnerable with them and I asked them to help me create a path forward and acknowledge that the business was in decline and that we were faced with a lot of risk and uncertainty. Most importantly, I told them that we would create a vision together of where the company was going to go in the future.

Remember how Hollis Harris, the former CEO of Continental Airlines, talked about risk and uncertainty in Chapter 2? He had the V (vulnerability) component of the equation but was missing the L (leadership) piece. Scott was in a very similar situation to Hollis in that the business was really struggling. Scott addressed the uncertainty and the risk head on, and although he didn't specify a solution he conveyed optimism, shared a vision, and rallied employees to come together to help him and the company reach that vision.

Being Authentic

One of the most common responses I got back from CEOs when I asked them what it means to be a vulnerable leader is being authentic. When I asked them what this means, they clarified that it's about just being you—the same version of yourself that you are at home as you are at work, with the same values, ideals, personality, and emotions.

Here's how Christian Klein, the CEO of the 110,00-person enterprise application software company SAP explained it to me: "The biggest mistake leaders make is that they think they have all the answers—and if they don't, they pretend they do. The truth is that no one on this planet knows all the answers. Be authentic. For people to trust you, you need to 'walk the talk' and shouldn't pretend to be someone you're not. If leaders can't be vulnerable, others on the team are not going to do that either."

For decades most of us had to live with two identities, like spies in an action thriller. We had the identity at home and the identity at work, and these two identities were never supposed to meet! Being authentic, simply put, means just being a single version of yourself.

Jeff Puritt is the president and CEO of TELUS International, a leading global digital customer experience provider with more than 70,000 employees. Several years ago when his leadership team came together, he and his colleagues around the table were invited to share something about themselves as an ice-breaker. A few individuals spoke before Jeff and shared very sterile and sanitized—arguably traditionally corporate environment appropriate stories. When it was Jeff's turn, he decided to talk about his daughter, Alexa (now 26 years old), who has a condition called BPAN, an ultra-rare genetic disorder that compromises protein processing in the body and adversely affects muscle and bone development, speech, and cognition. Alexa only learned to walk when she was five and to this day she has never spoken a word. She has to be cared for around the clock and is not able to live an independent life. My eyes welled up with tears when Jeff told me this story because I have a young daughter and I couldn't imagine going through what Jeff and his family have gone through.

What I found so powerful from Jeff's story is when he talked about the little things that bring his daughter joy, like driving in the car with the window open to feel the breeze in her hair or floating and playing in water. Jeff was candid in telling me that despite, or perhaps because of, his daughter's condition and limited life expectancy, his daughter inspires him every day.

Through her, he learned to never sweat the small things in life, to be grateful for what he has, and to live life to the fullest. He shared this experience with his leadership team that day to let them know that he is a human being with personal challenges and struggles, that he is an authentic leader and a single version of himself.

Showing Sincere Emotion

One CEO of a 42,000-person media company shared a very powerful story with me. She is the type of leader who wants to get to know her people. She spends time talking with them, learning about their families, their struggles, and their wins. But for this CEO it was always a one-way street. In other words, she allowed and encouraged other people to be vulnerable with her, but she was not vulnerable with them. One day, she received terrifying news. She had cancer. Fortunately, it was operable and it was caught early. She wanted to share the news with her team:

> I stood up in front of the team of 150 people in our cafeteria to tell them I was going to be off for a few weeks and let them know what was going on. I heard myself telling them a story of how lucky I was and that [what I had was] the best cancer to have if you're gonna have cancer, and that I'm going to be fine and it's not a big deal. I heard myself saying these things and I realized it's not authentic, I wasn't letting them in. I would encourage them to let me in, but I didn't do this for them. I stopped and I told them how scared I was and what I was worried about. I shared what I was nervous about both personally and professionally and that I was going to have to be gone for six weeks and I was scared for myself and the team.
>
> I came around the corner the day before I was leaving for surgery, and my desk was literally jammed with handwritten notes and cards from every single member of the team. I had a box of books, too. But it was more about the types of messages with people saying things like "you got this," "'you've had us all this time, it's our time to have you." The sentiment and what I got back out of being vulnerable, honest, and real with them was more than I'd ever given them. It was incredible. This experience taught me that I'm never going to pretend to

be anything else other than me. My team gave me what I really needed but had I not been vulnerable and asked for it, I wouldn't have ever gotten it and that support was really important to me during a tough time.

This is such a powerful story, and it really highlights one simple fact. We are all human and we need to take care of each other. It's okay to share emotions at work, whether those emotions are positive or negative, but remember the context of the environment you are in.

This means that it's okay to be upset, but if you need to take some time to collect yourself before attending a meeting, then do so, and if you're furious at someone, then go for a five-minute walk to calm down instead of throwing a chair across the room. Showing sincere emotion doesn't mean you shouldn't be able to emotionally regulate yourself.

Looking at the data, the top responses for how people convey they are feeling vulnerable to others at work are "admitting to a mistake" and "being authentic," which both scored at 83%. These were followed closely by "saying I don't know" at 73%, "asking for help" at 68%, and "showing sincere emotion" at 64%. By far, the lowest scoring response at 11% was "I expect others to see if I'm put in a vulnerable situation" (see Figure 11.2)

I was quite surprised by this last figure because it clearly shows that in the workplace we don't expect people to identify vulnerability unless it is expressly conveyed. However, situational vulnerability, such as being put on a tough project or reporting to a leader with a bad reputation, are clearly times that would make someone feel vulnerable. The fact that we don't expect others to notice when we are put in vulnerable situations is troublesome because it means we don't believe they have the capacity to do so, and it shouldn't be expected in a work setting. Neither of these are positive.

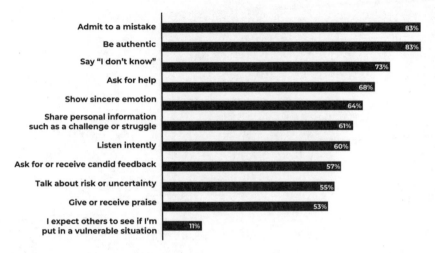

Figure 11.2 Which of the following are the best examples of how you convey feeling vulnerable to others?

These are the 10 vulnerability signs. However, there's one large caveat when it comes to paying attention to the vulnerability signs, and that's what Chapter 12 is about.

12

It Takes One to Know One

In 1995, a heavyset man in his mid-40s robbed two Pittsburgh banks in broad daylight. He didn't wear a mask or a disguise of any kind, and in fact he smiled at the security cameras filming him. The footage from the security camera was broadcast across media and news outlets across the city and that very evening he was arrested. As McArthur Wheeler was being placed in handcuffs he shockingly cried, "But I wore the juice!"

At first police thought that he might be crazy or on drugs, but that wasn't the case. McArthur was simply mistaken. He believed that by rubbing lemon juice on his face he would be invisible to security cameras. If you write a message on paper using lemon juice, the message will disappear; if you apply a heat source like a light bulb to the paper, the message will reappear. Because lemon juice can be used as invisible ink, Mr. Wheeler believed it would make him invisible, too.

This story immediately caught the attention of Dr. David Dunning and one of his graduate students, Dr. Justin Kruger. Together they developed a theory in psychology that became known as the Dunning-Kruger effect, which states that people with a low experience, ability, or expertise in a certain area oftentimes overestimate their abilities in that area. Put another way, people who are incompetent at something don't have the skills or abilities to know that they are incompetent to begin with!

Translating this to being a vulnerable leader, it means that if you are not vulnerable yourself, then you will not be able to tell if someone is being vulnerable with you because you don't have that competency to begin with.

Here's what Dr. Dunning told me, which is profound and insightful:

> It's hard to know when a person might be vulnerable if you haven't had experiences and thoughtful reflection about what's made you vulnerable. You have to know about the dynamics of situations and circumstances, how they're going to make a person feel, and if they will make someone feel vulnerable or not. If you have done that, then you'll be able to recognize the other person may very well be in a vulnerable state. If you don't have that, you're not going to be able to recognize that they're in a vulnerable state. On top of that, you won't know that you don't know.
>
> A lot of our understanding of other people is really coming to understand ourselves. That is, we're all more alike than we are different. For readers of this book to best come to an understanding of vulnerability and others—When is it going to happen? What are the effects? If it needs to be repaired, how do you repair it?—really comes from understanding yourself and what will work with you or what's happened to you in the past. That is one of the best data points in a lot of different areas of life in dealing with another person. Think about yourself and your own experiences with vulnerability; it can turn out to be an incredibly valid indicator for you to figure out the dynamics of what's going on and what to do.

This is an important point to remember because who is to say if you are vulnerable or not? There is no objective criteria or scoring for this. You may do something you believe is making you vulnerable but those around you don't see it that way. It's a bit like that philosophical thought experiment: "If a tree falls in the woods and nobody is around to hear it, does it make a sound?" Similarly, if you believe you are being vulnerable with someone but they don't perceive that vulnerability, are you being vulnerable?"

To identify when someone might be feeling vulnerable or be in a vulnerable situation, you need to have some experience with vulnerability yourself, which everyone in the world has had whether that vulnerability was experienced personally or in the workplace.

Dr. Dunning makes a very important distinction, though, and that is being able to reflect on what makes you vulnerable and what that feels like. I asked CEOs questions such as "What makes you feel most vulnerable at work and why?" and "What does vulnerability feel like?" They all had answers to these questions but it took them some time to reflect, collect their thoughts, and respond.

It's not that we aren't familiar with vulnerability or don't have experience with it—we do. It's just that these aren't things we usually spend time thinking or talking about.

Sal A. Abbate, the CEO of Veritiv who met in Chapter 8, had an awkward experience with a leader earlier in his career who tried to show vulnerability, and it was very obvious to everyone on the team that he wasn't being authentic:

> I had a really tough and hard-nosed boss earlier in my career when I worked for a company in the transportation industry. I was a 19-year-old intern at the company and he called a few of us together into his office and then he started playing "Wind Beneath My Wings" by Bette Midler. He started telling us that we were the wind beneath his wings and we all just looked at each other and thought he was having some kind of a nervous breakdown. It was so out of his character and didn't feel natural that we didn't take it seriously and

thought there was something wrong with him. This caused him more harm than good. We'd rather have the predictable guy who we knew was going to kick us in the teeth because at least we knew that guy.

Being vulnerable isn't something you can just flip a switch to activate. As in Sal's case, if as a leader you act in a way that doesn't align with who your people think you are, then it creates confusion. It takes time and communication to learn how to lead with vulnerability.

13

I Saw the Sign!

If you're going down a winding road and you see a sign warning you to slow down to 30 miles per hour when making the turns, you slow down. Similarly, when you see a vulnerability sign, the smart thing to do is pay attention to it and become more aware of your surroundings and how the other person might be feeling. These signs should tingle your vulnerability spidey senses. Sometimes these signs are just that—signs that don't turn into anything or don't manifest. However, sometimes these signs will be very useful guides to help you and those around you.

Ilham Kadri is the CEO of Solvay, a 21,000-person chemical company. She was raised in Morocco by her illiterate grandmother who told her that young girls had two choices or exits in life. One from her parents' home to her husband's home and the other to the grave. Ilham found her third exit in the form of education. She spent many years studying and working around the world, ultimately getting her PhD and becoming the CEO of Diversey in the US and now of Solvay in Belgium. She is also the chair of the nonprofit World Business Council for Sustainable Development. Ilham also suffers from dyslexia, which made it particularly challenging for her to achieve her current level of success. Despite all of these obstacles, she conquered everything thrown her way, and vulnerability was a crucial element of her success, not just in terms of how she practiced it but also in terms of how she responded to others when they were vulnerable with her:

> If someone is vulnerable with you, then you need to detect and be able to understand what is really being said or asked of you. Anyone can say, "Please help me," and it's easy to just pay attention to the words, but the context and meaning of those words matters much more. Is the person in some kind of distress? Is their job on the line? Are they personally and/or professionally struggling? Are they in some kind of a difficult situation? Looking for the vulnerability signs is a powerful way of trying to understand what vulnerability is being expressly stated and what is under the surface. You need to be extremely open-minded, emotionally available, and present. If someone is vulnerable with you, you need to engage in a way that conveys empathy, respect, support, and a willingness to listen and help. I often say, "I am one phone call away from you." A good leader is a caring, empathetic human being who connects with others at a human level.

Most of the discussions about vulnerability focus on the person being vulnerable. But the person who is receiving, observing, or identifying vulnerability in someone else has a lot of responsibility and power. Consider some of the stories you have already read in these pages about when leaders either had vulnerability backfire or used against them. These things happened because the other person made a poor and hurtful choice. When someone is vulnerable with you, you, too, have a choice.

Nicholas Fink is the CEO of Fortune Brands Home & Security Inc., which has more than 28,000 employees. Here's what he shared with me: "It's very humbling when someone is vulnerable with me at work and shares a challenge, a struggle, or what is going on in their life. Essentially what they are doing is giving me the gift of truth, and I try to model that same behavior. It's the most powerful gift anyone can give you."

The simple answer to what to do when you notice a vulnerability sign or when someone is directly vulnerable with you is don't be a jerk (you can replace *jerk* with your word of choice). Life is short; we all go through challenges and even if you have the opportunity to stick it to someone, don't. This is where the Golden Rule comes in: treat the other person the way you want to be treated.

One CEO of a mid-size technology company who chose to remain anonymous told me an interesting story of when he worked at one of the world's largest technology companies:

> I'm a competitive person and I was going for a general manager job that my boss at the time had promised me after he would be promoted to CEO. I worked my ass off for years and finally thought I was going to get what was due to me. When he got the CEO role he said, "I'm sorry the job is going to go to Jane." I said, "What the fuck? She doesn't know anything about the business!" He just came back and said that's the way it has to be.
>
> I accepted it but I didn't make Jane's life easy and I didn't like her very much. She was sandwiched between me and the CEO, who was my advocate, which put her in a very difficult, almost impossible situation. I thought she would eventually quit and I'd take her job. I would do things like go around her to speak with her boss to get approvals and do things without telling her. This went on for a few years and, of course, she never quit. I ended up moving to a new team and working on something else. One day the CEO got fired and I realized that I needed an ally at the company and I thought of Jane, who had always been good to me and she was at my level in the company.
>
> I went to Jane and did a little bit of soul searching. I talked to her and said, "I know how much of a difficult situation I put you in and how that must have impacted you. I made your life difficult and I'm really sorry for doing that." She looked at me

and then burst into tears and I teared up as well. I was like, holy shit, I had no idea the impact that I had on this other human being. I always assumed she was like the ice queen with no feeling or emotion. My whole life came crashing down like a house of cards because I realized everything I had been doing was all about my own self-importance.

By being vulnerable with Jane and apologizing for how I treated her and acknowledging the suffering I had caused her, I was able to build a new relationship with her, one that continues to this day where we are now friends, and I even asked her to join my board.

Throughout all of this Jane was always kind and respectful to this person, even though he was torturing her, which must have been incredibly difficult for her. She put on a brave face and soldiered on as many women have to do (several of those stories are in this book). Oftentimes we don't realize the impact we have on others. We assume everyone around us is tough and can take whatever we put them through because that is the stereotype of leadership. This now CEO had to put his ego aside and embrace vulnerable leadership with Jane, something that takes courage and reflection. As this leader told me, this experience has forever changed his life.

Tooey Courtemanche is the CEO of Procore technologies, a construction software company with more than 3,000 employees. He shared a story with me of how vulnerability didn't connect with someone on his team:

I have loving parents but I was brought up in a house where the kids sat at the kids' table and spoke when they were spoken to. My best friend from seventh grade, who is still my best friend today, had parents who were intellectual; one was a lawyer and the other was a doctor, and I would beg my parents to eat dinner at their house because over there the kids sat with the adults and the adults engaged the kids in intellectual conversations, and they would ask us our opinions on things. I felt valued and that people cared about my voice. I want everyone I work with to feel that way and being a vulnerable leader is how I do it. But one time it actually backfired on me.

I had somebody who worked for me several years ago who did not like my leadership style of vulnerability. This person was looking for a command-and-control leader and actually wanted someone with an ego who could tell them what the most important thing was and how to do their job. They were raised in a family where vulnerability was seen as weakness and so they viewed me as a weak leader. I actually didn't realize that my vulnerability was creating problems until one day they gave me very direct feedback and criticism and said I was a weak leader by being vulnerable. This person actually asked me point-blank one day, "Why aren't you just giving me the answer?" I told them that wasn't my style. I don't see my vulnerability as weakness. We don't work together anymore and this is why I now hire for three attributes, which are hungry, smart, and humble.

Tooey also told me that had he not been vulnerable, he would have never even started his company to begin with.

You have tremendous power and responsibility when someone is vulnerable with you. If you don't feel comfortable reciprocating vulnerability, which not everyone does, then at the very least you should make the other person feel seen and valued. The best piece of advice I have when someone is being vulnerable with you is don't be a jerk. This choice can be as simple as a smile or a nod during a tense meeting or saying, "I'm proud of the work you did even though we didn't get the deal."

It's never your place to share someone else's vulnerability and it's not okay to use someone else's vulnerability against them. What would this say about you as a person and is that the message you want everyone around you to get? You live once; be good to your fellow humans.

14

The Sprinter and the Gymnast

In 2009, Berlin hosted the World Championships in Athletics. At the 100-meter sprint, athletes from around the world who had trained their entire lives lined up ready to see who would be the world's fastest man. The gun went off and less than 10 seconds later Usain Bolt crossed the finish line with a world record time of 9.58 seconds that still stands today. The second-place finisher was just 0.13 seconds behind Usain. Even though it was a very close race there was no question who won; Usain clearly crossed the finish line first.

Věra Čáslavská was a Czech gymnast who won 22 international titles between 1959 and 1968, including an astounding seven Olympic gold medals. She is considered to be one of the world's greatest gymnasts. At the 1968 Olympic games, Věra was performing a balance beam routine in front of judges from Hungary, Russia, Poland, the United States, and what at the time was known as East Germany. She scored 9.65, which gave her the silver medal. Her performance was perceived by the audience as perfect, and so her lower score was met with confusion, arguments, massive protest, and uproar in the arena. This lasted more than 10 minutes, at which point her score was increased to 9.8. Even though she got the silver medal, everyone thought she deserved gold and nobody understood why she didn't get it. There were a few problems with the subjective scoring. First, one of the judges was from Russia, which at the time had just invaded Czechoslovakia, and Věra was a strong opponent of Soviet leadership and communism. Second, the Russian judge actually lost to Věra in a previous Olympic competition. Third, the Russian judge was captain of the Soviet national team and was also judging her former teammates from prior years. All of this created a massive conflict of interest. On top of all of this, the judges couldn't agree on the deductions to give Věra based on where she was placing her hands on the beam to balance herself.[1]

Sprinting is an objective sport. It's very clear who the winner is: it's the person who crosses the finish line first, an objective reality. Gymnastics is a subjective sport in which the athletes need to worry about what goes into the judges' minds. This makes for a whole new level of pressure, nerves, and anxiety. At work, we are all gymnasts.

Dr. Thomas Gilovich is a professor at Cornell University and is considered one of the world's leading social psychologists. He did some research in which he interviewed athletes who competed in both types of sports: those when the outcome is determined by judges and those when the outcome is determined by objective metrics (higher, faster, longer). When the athletes were asked which sport they were more nervous for beforehand, the overwhelming majority stated before the events in which the outcome was determined by judges.

This is one of the challenges when it comes to vulnerability, especially in a leadership context. There is a fear of judgment because the reality is not objective. The truth is we have no idea how someone will respond to our willingness to be vulnerable or if they even perceive our vulnerability. There is no clear metric and no objective reality.

If every leader knew that if they shared a mistake they made that it would create more trust, engagement, and a positive perception, then they would do it. But that is not the case. As a leader you are a gymnast appearing before other human beings with subjective realities. This creates a high level of uncertainty, which we generally don't like.

The good news is that unlike an Olympic sport when your score is final, in life and in the workplace it isn't. If you are vulnerable with someone at work and things don't go well, you have choices. For example, you can try to identify why what you said or did wasn't received in the intended way and then try to correct it, or you can determine if the relationship is one worth pursuing, if the other person is willing to get to know the real you.

One powerful and simple technique you can use to get more clarification and insights is the follow-up (see Figure 14.1). When my seven-year-old daughter Naomi asks me for more dessert and I say "no," she never responds back with "Okay, that makes sense." Instead, I get follow-ups such as "How come?" or "Didn't I eat enough dinner?" She always has a follow-up to that *no* with the intention of getting what she wants or understanding why she didn't get what she wanted. Similarly, if you're being vulnerable with someone when you care about the relationship and you can sense that things aren't being received the right way, don't just accept that experience as a *no*. Follow up to get more information and insight, and remember to add the L to being vulnerable (V). In this case that L would be a learning moment to find out why things didn't connect the right way and what you can do to improve.

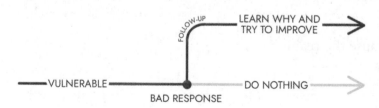

Figure 14.1 The follow-up

Imagine if you were a gymnast competing at the Olympics and after your first routine you had the opportunity to sit down with the judges and ask them questions, not just about your routine but about how they perceived you and felt about you and what you could do differently from both a technical and also an emotional perspective to get a higher score. Well, you can do that at work and in your personal life by following up and asking questions or saying things such as these:

- "I shared something pretty personal earlier and I wasn't sure it came across the right way. How did you interpret what I said?"
- "Did you think the way I talked about my mistake during the meeting sounded weird?"
- "Sometimes I can be pretty open about my personal and professional life. If that makes you uncomfortable, then please let me know."

Don't overthink the follow-up; just do what comes naturally to get some clarification and further insight. It's important to accept and understand that we are all human and we all want to be perceived in a positive light. You're a gymnast, not a sprinter, and so is everyone else around you.

Being judged can be a scary thing. We all judge and we are all judged and in extreme cases, a fear of judgment leads to anxiety disorders. This is why avoiding judging others is so important. Let's say you go to a restaurant with a friend and your waiter isn't particularly friendly. He seems irritated, doesn't smile when he talks to you, accidentally spills some water on your shirt, and gives off that "I don't want to serve you" vibe.

I've certainly experienced that before as I'm sure you have. What goes through your mind in that situation? You're probably thinking, "This waiter is a complete jerk. I'm going to speak with his manager, and I hope he gets fired. I'll show him!"

But how come you aren't thinking, "This poor guy must be having a really rough day, maybe his girlfriend left him, perhaps his mom is really sick, or maybe his boss just yelled at him. I hope everything is okay and that things turn around for him."

According to a theory in psychology called fundamental attribution error, we assume that the way a person behaves is as a result of who they are instead of the circumstance or situation they might be in. We also tend to excuse our own behavior and give ourselves a break when we are faced with a similar situation.

But the truth is that in many situations, the way a person behaves has nothing to do with who they are but with the circumstances they are faced with. Instead of being quick to judge someone you can try to remove judgment by trying to think of something that may have caused that person to act the way they did.

This all comes from our desire to feel a sense of belonging at work, which is not possible without vulnerability. Belonging means you feel like you are a part of something greater than yourself. In the context of this book, it means you are a part of a team or a company that encourages you to be yourself. It's a catch-22. We all want to feel like we belong, but most of us don't feel like we can be vulnerable at work, which is what creates belonging to begin with.

Barbara Humpton is the president and CEO of Siemens USA, which employs more than 40,000 people in the company's largest global market. Earlier on in her career she was told that she would never be able to be a senior executive and that she would have to choose between being a mom or a leader: "I was told senior leadership is not a career path for me. I accepted it because back in the day that's what you did and you just go on with your career. Then, lo and behold, one day I got invited to do a big job and the big question I had in my mind was, 'Am I ready to do this?'"

Barbara was working at IBM, which then sold its business serving the federal government to Lockheed Martin. During this transition, "IBM-slash-Lockheed Martin," as Barbara put it, was supporting the US Air Force on a complex project that was foundational to the development of the global positioning system, or GPS.

"The phone rang," Barbara recalled, "and I'm asked to take over as the new project manager." For Barbara, this was a fantastic opportunity, a steppingstone to executive management. At the same time, the project was already two years in the making, behind schedule, and over budget. Barbara accepted the assignment and, as she walked into a meeting with the leadership team, she felt everyone lock eyes on her with facial expressions that said, "Who is she to guide us out of this mess we're in?" She felt "imposter syndrome" creep in. "I knew this was day one of a new journey for me, and it did not feel good. I knew I was being judged before I even said anything." In fact, as she introduced herself to members of the team, Barbara remembers one person coming up to her and asking her if she was the "new guy." "He then pointed to one of his colleagues and said, 'This is the last new guy we had and he's been here for 19 years.' That felt really vulnerable."

At that moment Barbara could have taken the role of the stereotypical leader. She could have gained control over the situation by asserting dominance and using the power of her seniority to force action. Barbara could have told everyone in the room that she was going to make big changes and had everything figured out. Instead, she tapped into the vulnerability she was feeling. She acknowledged that this was a difficult assignment, that she didn't have all of the answers, and that even though she was the senior leader in the room, she was there to learn from others instead of expecting that others would just comply with her orders.

> I told everyone there that I want to learn from them and that I know I need to work hard to earn trust, build relationships, and gain credibility. Most leaders assume these things but the reality is that these are things leaders must earn. Those first few days, weeks, and months were a bit of the team testing me to see how I would behave. One by one I learned about all of

the leaders and what each of them brought to the table. I built relationships with the influencers in that room who would help everyone else accept me and help us succeed as a team.

Barbara was able to turn the project around and today, this experience helps her navigate similar situations.

Think of our ancestors. Being judged favorably was ultimately what led to the success of many while being judged unfavorably led to having your head lopped off. Thankfully we've come a long way since then but for many of us it does come back to that survival instinct, which is, good judgment means survival and thriving, whereas bad judgment means ridicule or death.

We learn this at an early age. I notice that even my daughter Naomi is talking about judgment and perception from others. Every morning for the past year my children and I have started doing daily affirmations in the car. I do this to instill a positive mindset in Naomi and my three-year-old son Noah.

Each morning as I'm driving my kids to school Naomi proudly exclaims, "I am strong, I am confident, I am brave, lots of people love me, I love myself, and I can do anything!" After she finishes we all do a little cheer in the car. Then Noah does his affirmation where he usually copies his big sister and then I do my own affirmation in front of my kids, which is usually, "I am patient, I am loving, I am kind, I am present, and I love myself." Sometimes our affirmations change depending on how we are feeling but these have been an important part of our morning routine.

Positive self-talk can dramatically shift your mindset and improve your performance and ability to connect with others. It requires practice and patience. Remind yourself that although you're not perfect, you're worth it.

15

What We Got Wrong About Milgram's Experiment

One of the world's most famous psychology experiments was conducted by Stanley Milgram starting in the 1960s. The experiment was designed to test obedience and involved three participants. The first was the experimenter, who acted as the authority figure running the experiment. Next was the teacher, who was the subject of the experiment. Last, was the learner, who pretended to be another subject in the experiment, but in reality was an actor.

Here's how the experiment looked.

At the beginning of the experiment, volunteers were introduced to another participant (the actor) and they drew a sheet of paper to see who would play the role of the teacher or the learner. The truth was that both sheets of paper said the same thing on it and the actor would just lie and say he got the role of the learner, so each time the volunteer would be the teacher but they thought it was by chance.

After the roles were assigned the learner was taken into an adjacent room and strapped into something that looked like an electric chair.

The volunteer, aka the teacher, and the experimenter then went into another room where a switchboard was labeled with various switches, each designed to deliver an electric shock ranging from "slight shock" up to "danger: severe shock." Before starting, the volunteer was given a very small shock so they could see that everything was indeed real. But, of course, no shocks were actually given to the learner in the other room (who the volunteer couldn't see, just hear).

Once everything was set up, the volunteer would then read out a set of word pairs, for example, he would say, "clear" goes with "air," or "dictionary" goes with "red." Then the learner (actor) would have to remember what the word pair was, every time he got it wrong, the volunteer was instructed to deliver an electric shock to the actor. Even though no electrical shocks were being administered the actor in the other room would grunt, shout with pain, say he didn't want to participate anymore, or even claim they had a heart condition!

The test was to see if the volunteer would keep administering electric shocks going all the way up to the potentially lethal 450-volt maximum. Whenever the volunteer would try to object or refuse to give further shocks the experimenter (authority figure) would respond with phrases such as, "The experiment requires you to go on" or "You have no choice. You must go on."

Almost 70% of the participants delivered the maximum level of shock. This experiment shocked (pun intended) the world because it was assumed that most people would stop when they found out they were hurting someone.

Like most of you reading this book, I assumed this experiment was simply exploring blind obedience but it's not. As Dr. Gilovich, whom I mentioned before, pointed out to me in our interview, there was nothing blind about it. In fact, if you watch the videos of these interviews you can clearly see that participants were trying to disobey. The subjects who were administering the shocks felt so uncomfortable that they started nervously laughing or smiling, tearing their hair out, digging their nails into their arms, and three of them had uncontrollable seizures.

They were so concerned with the awkwardness of the situation and how they would be perceived that they participated in what Dr. Gilovich refers to as ineffective and indecisive disobedience.

How people perceive us plays an important role in the decisions we make and how we act. When we imagine others being vulnerable, we think of how brave and courageous they are, but when we imagine ourselves being vulnerable, we tend to immediately jump to the negative. Just like in Milgram's experiment, we are concerned with how we are perceived, regarded, and judged by others. Milgram's experiment shows us what happens not when we blindly obey but when we let other people's perceptions of us dictate how we behave.

Tina Freese Decker is the president and CEO of Corewell Health, a health product company with more than 60,000 team members. When we spoke, she shared a story with me about how someone told her she needed to be more aggressive and assertive in meetings. This isn't her personality. Tina is much more collaborative, engaging, and wants everyone to feel comfortable and heard. But, she went against her better judgment and took this person's advice. During a negotiation meeting she wasn't creating an environment that she or other people felt comfortable with and she could tell she was losing everyone: "It was not me, and I immediately regretted taking that advice. The outcome wasn't good, either. But when I think of that experience now, I realize that person whose advice I took actually helped me. I tried being someone I'm not, and I am never going to do it again. I learned from it and I won't apply that to any situation again."

In the middle of the meeting Tina realized what was going on; she could tell by looking at the body language and expressions of those around her that nothing was resonating. She decided to go back to her usual self:

> It's hard to recover when you're in a meeting to switch, but I stopped going down that path. And I tried to back up a little to make sure we could get a better outcome. Because you could tell that both sides of the negotiation were just going to dig in,

so I made the decision to come back and figure out how we can get back together and find an outcome that would work. You have to go back to who you are, what you stand for, your values and what your brand is, and make sure you're consistent.

In 1987, a psychologist by the name of Edward Torry Higgins proposed the self-discrepancy theory, which explores how likely we are to experience emotional distress when we hold incompatible or conflicting views and beliefs about ourselves. According to Dr. Torry Higgins, we all have three versions of ourselves. The actual self is who we believe we are, the ideal self is who we want to be, and the ought self is who others want us to be. According to the self-discrepancy theory, when we see inconsistencies and large gaps between these perceptions, we start to experience emotional distress and discomfort.

For example, you may have an ideal version of yourself as a leader in which you are strong, confident, knowledgeable, and decisive. You may have an ought version of yourself as a leader in which you need to connect with your people and get to know them as human beings. However, your actual self may be someone who is just mediocre at both and doesn't really live up to either of these expectations. These discrepancies can lead to feelings such as imposter syndrome, lack of engagement, frustration, burnout, and other negative emotional and cognitive challenges.

Louis Tremblay is the president and CEO of FLO, a manufacturer and network operator of electric vehicle charging solutions. He gave me the perfect example of this:

The ideal version of myself doesn't make mistakes, is 100% himself when he is in conflict, and inspires his people while giving them clear guidance. This version of me also understands that I need competitors because together we are fighting for a bigger mission of fighting climate change. The mission is more important than all of us. The ideal version of me is also a great father and husband who is always present for his family. My actual self wants to crush my competitors and sometimes overlooks the broader mission to focus on being number one. I also make mistakes regularly and have weeks where my balance of work and life is absolutely terrible, and I know I'm not present for my family the way I should be. There is a gap between these two versions of me which can cause me to feel stressed, anxious, and uneasy.

If we show up to work each day believing we need to always have the answers, not show emotion, avoid sharing any mistakes or failures, and act like a robot when we know that is not who we really are, then of course that is going to create emotional challenges for us. It becomes that much more difficult to actually challenge these versions of our "ideal selves." To lead a fulfilling professional and personal life means to embrace your imperfections and the imperfections of those around you. The alternative is trying to strive for the unattainable, which will only lead to a negative outcome.

It's far more effective to change the conversation to focus on what you can do to learn and grow as a leader. If you can improve by 1% a day, then by the end of the year you will be 37× better.

Sometimes leading with vulnerability is awkward and clumsy. Leaders have all sorts of playbooks for how to deal with various situations. There's no playbook for being a human being, and sometimes you're going to screw up. As you saw in Tina's example, she knew she wasn't being herself and quickly pivoted when she realized that.

In the study "Fostering Perceptions of Authenticity via Sensitive Self-Disclosure," the authors found that when leaders are voluntarily open about their flaws and weaknesses, they create more authenticity with their people. The more senior the leader is, the greater the positive impacts are, specifically concerning trustworthiness.[1]

Don't assume that being vulnerable will result in other people seeing you in a negative light.[2] Often the truth is the exact opposite.

16

The Four Types of Questions

What makes you feel most vulnerable at work? Is it when you need to ask for help? Perhaps it's when you are receiving candid feedback from someone you trust? Or maybe it's when you have to genuinely admit to a mistake?

This is one of the questions I asked the over 100 CEOs I interviewed. My idea was to create a kind of vulnerability scale. On the lower end of the scale would be something like asking for help and on the high end of the scale would be something like admitting to a huge mistake. The idea was to show what makes leaders feel less and most vulnerable and then give some tools based on where someone falls on the scale.

This sounds like a pretty straightforward and valuable framework to create, or so I thought. Here are a few of the responses I received from CEOs when asked "What makes you feel most vulnerable at work?"

"When I have to bring to life mistakes I have made that have hurt other people, made them uncomfortable, or somehow made their lives more difficult."

—Zig Serafin, CEO of Qualtrics
(more than 5,000 employees)

"When I feel very strongly that a decision needs to be made or a pivot has to occur that the rest of the leadership team doesn't see or believe. I'm a collaborative person by nature so having to challenge my team and tell them we need to do something is really hard."

—Sheryl Palmer, CEO of Taylor Morrison
(3,000 employees)

"The absence of people I can talk to and trust. Oftentimes when making decisions you have access to a team of people you can rely on for insights and advice. But sometimes it can be very lonely to be a CEO because eventually you need to make the decision and you can't always get the opinion of the group or you don't have access to other people whom you can trust. Feeling alone when making decisions is something I find to be very vulnerable."

—Gonzalo Gortázar, CEO,
CaixaBank (45,000 employees)

"Speaking about or presenting about a topic that is outside of my core area of expertise. I would question how I'm representing myself and my firm, if I should have prepared more, or if I should be speaking about that topic to begin with."

—Alison Martin, CEO EMEA (Europe, Middle East,
and Africa) and Bank Distribution of Zurich Insurance Group
(55,000 employees; Alison leads about half of them)

"As the CEO I sometimes feel like I need to know everything and master everything, which is not realistic. When I have to rely on someone else or a team to handle something important in the right way, that can make me feel very vulnerable because I feel it should be my responsibility. In my role I can't possibly know or do everything, which is something I have come to accept."

—CEO of a large consumer packaged goods company
(118,000 employees)

"When I have to make a decision that negatively impacts the lives of others, especially those on the ground floor making our products and getting them out. As an organization, we have an obligation to our entire team and their families. When I make decisions that impact them negatively, that's more emotional to me than if a decision impacts a senior executive. And that's because those are the people that make the business run every day."

—Edward Pesicka, president and CEO, Owens & Minor
(17,000 employees)

These responses confused me. The CEOs all shared different stories and examples with me, and I didn't see a clear pattern, which meant that I couldn't create a vulnerability scale.

I quickly realized that what makes leaders (and all of us) feel vulnerable is very subjective. If you take a look at the four examples I just shared (and I have countless others), you will see that they are all different yet they are all things that make these leaders feel most vulnerable. The responses seemed to be all over the map and ranged from speaking on a stage, to hiring or firing someone, to listening, to receiving praise, to showing any kind of emotion, to talking about life outside of work.

If different things make us feel vulnerable, then how could I possibly make sense of all of the responses? I almost gave up, but then I had an idea . . . and it all came down to a single word, *why?*

The question became, "What makes you feel most vulnerable at work and why?"

That is when I discovered two profound insights. The first is that leaders feel vulnerable when they are forced to ask themselves one of four types of questions. These are questions of the mind (thoughts), questions of the body (actions), questions of the heart (feelings), and questions of the soul (who you are).

It's analogous to chess. Oftentimes when playing against an opponent, you make a move that forces them to ask a question, such as "Where are you going to move your piece now that I attacked it?" or "I don't think your attack has any merit; show me how you're going to checkmate me!"

Vulnerability can be felt in different parts of the body as well. Hubert Joly is the former chairman and CEO of Best Buy and is responsible for one of the greatest business turnarounds in modern corporate history. When everyone thought he was crazy for taking over the company and predicted failure and bankruptcy, he led his 100,000 employees to success.

One of the most powerful things I've learned as a leader over the past two years is that we need to lead with all parts of our body. This also means you can feel vulnerability in different parts of the body. Vulnerability of the mind means you question an idea or you don't know something so you go look for help and find the answer. Vulnerability of the body means that you question an action so you will need to decide if it's an action worth standing by or one that merits a change. Vulnerability of the heart is much different. You might not feel respected, seen, or heard. Rene Descartes said, "I think, therefore I am." He was wrong. He should have said, "I am seen, therefore I am." If I'm not feeling seen, I will feel vulnerable, I will feel lost. The deepest type of vulnerability is in the soul. This is when something touches your very existence and makes you question who you are as a person and as a leader. It's crucial for leaders to understand these four areas and questions they can ask when feeling vulnerable so that they connect with themselves and those around them.

The second insight is that for every single CEO I interviewed, what makes them feel *most* vulnerable is when they are forced to question who they are as a leader or person, that is, their soul.

This is a difficult thing to get clarity in because it can be different for everyone. Remember that carnival game where you have to hit a lever as hard as you can with a sledgehammer to get a puck to rise to the top so it rings a bell? Everyone has a different threshold of how high that puck needs to go before they feel vulnerable.

These are the four types of questions that make leaders feel vulnerable at work (see Figure 16.1).

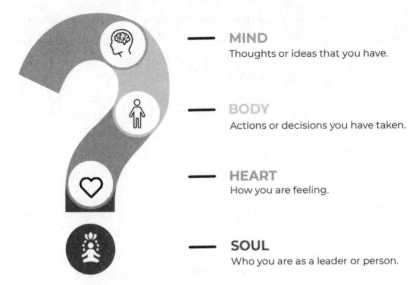

MIND
Thoughts or ideas that you have.

BODY
Actions or decisions you have taken.

HEART
How you are feeling.

SOUL
Who you are as a leader or person.

Figure 16.1 The Four types of questions

Questions of the Mind

In a work environment, we're often asked to share our thoughts and even defend them. Have you ever been in a meeting where you were asked to share your thoughts on a particular subject only to see that those around you didn't find value or merit in what you were sharing? Or perhaps your peers just didn't agree with your way of thinking? This is a vulnerable place to be in, especially if you are a leader. Maybe you are even questioning your own thoughts!

Here are some examples of questioning your thoughts:

- Sharing an idea that doesn't land well with others, which makes you question why you had that thought to begin with
- Feeling self-conscious about a new idea you have so you never share it with others, then berating yourself about it

- Realizing you don't know something or need help with something and then having to take the necessary steps to close that knowledge gap, which can make you question why you don't know something

Ilham Kadri, whom we met in Chapter 13, has had to question many of her thoughts: "I have dyslexia so it sometimes feels like my thoughts are a wide river I cannot control; and I'm sitting in a tiny rowboat trying to get through it, for instance, searching for a word or speaking.

"While I'm rowing in the river, sometimes I catch the flow and sometimes my boat can get overturned. With practice, hard work, and going slow to go fast, I could help myself."

There is no one-size-fits-all approach here and not all thoughts you question will make you feel vulnerable. Even when writing this book, I had all sorts of thoughts about the themes I wanted to explore. Some of them felt more vulnerable to question, for example, my family story at the beginning of the book or even some of the frameworks I developed. When I first decided I wanted to write this book, all I had was an idea and a very rough set of questions that I wanted to explore. When I finally signed the contract, the book became real and I realized that the ideas and questions I had about vulnerability were things that I now needed to face and confront head on. That's when my panic attacks began, when I realized that there was no more hiding from vulnerability.

There are lots of thoughts that you can question, and for many leaders, it makes them feel vulnerable.

Questions of the Body

One of the things that truly sets leaders apart is the impact they have on those around them. This can be a team, a function, a company, a community, or the world at large. This impact largely comes in the form of actions that leaders take. For example, a leader can mandate that everyone come back to the office post-pandemic, invest millions of dollars into a local community, or decide to create a new product or service that the company offers. Not every action a leader takes is going to be the right one or the best one. When leaders question an action they took, it can make them feel vulnerable.

Questions of the body can include scenarios such as the following:

- Hiring or firing someone
- Presenting during a company town hall
- Recognizing a team member
- Creating a new team
- Asking a question at a team meeting

The list of actions leaders take is, of course, extensive and never-ending.

Jeff Puritt, whom we met in Chapter 11, shared the following:

I absolutely made a bad hire and even though it happened over a decade ago, the consequence of it still troubles/haunts me today greatly. I let someone lead the largest part of our business and within six months he had fired several of our longest-tenured, loyal, and capable team members under the guise of them not being fit for purpose, not recognizing his leadership, and undermining his authority. Having hired him and he being so highly recommended and qualified, I sat back and thought "Well, perhaps he knows better than I do." This was really vulnerable for me because I treat my business like my family, and I feel very emotionally connected to my colleagues. I truly regret that I ever hired this person because I lost so many amazing people. The business struggled under his leadership and it wasn't until I exited and replaced him and built that team back up that we returned to a growth trajectory and we've been on that path ever since he left. To this day I still question and lament why I ever hired him, and I work diligently to avoid repeating that mistake.

Questions of the Heart

Questioning how you feel is not effective or, in many cases, even possible if you don't have the language required to answer that question for yourself. In other words, as a leader are you able to take a step back and actually ask "How am I feeling right now?" and do you have the language to answer that question?

This is something I shared previously in the book. If you can't identify emotions, then you will struggle with trying to understand what you are feeling and even why you are feeling it.

Questions of the heart include feelings such as the following:

- Not feeling respected, seen, or heard
- Struggling with imposter syndrome where you feel like you don't belong
- Believing you are isolated and alone with nobody to help you

Hal Lawton is the president and CEO of Tractor Supply Company, which has almost 50,000 employees. He shared some great insight with me on this during our interview and provided a fantastic visual that I've since started using in my life.

There's this one technique that I've done with a coach where you ground yourself in your various inner personalities, especially the one that relates to imposter syndrome, which makes you question how you feel about yourself and if you belong. For many of us, that inner critic is a very loud voice and it's elbowing out some of those other internal personalities that you have, and it's always telling you that you can't do it and that you won't level up. It creates self-doubt. This is the personality you need to make peace with, just like you would a good friend. You move them to the other corner of the room or table so you can let the other positive personalities sit with you and play to the moment you need.

Hal's technique is both simple and powerful, and it's not about deleting your negative personality; it's about giving it a seat in the room, just not at the center with your positive personalities.

Questions of the Soul

This last question is unique. In 100% of all of my CEO interviews, leaders feel most vulnerable when they have to ask themselves this question. This question can arrive either on its own or it can happen as a result of one of the previous three questions. Whatever path leads to this question, the outcome is the same. When a leader is forced to question who they are as a person or as a leader, they feel most vulnerable.

This can be different for everyone. It can be hiring the wrong person for a job or leaving someone in a role for too long when it's clear they aren't a good fit. It can be making a strategic decision that ends up backfiring or it can be having a meaningful one-on-one conversation with someone. We all have different levers and thresholds of vulnerability, but questioning who you are as a person and a leader sits at the very top of that threshold. Only you will know what makes you ask this question and why.

Lara Abrash is the Chair of Deloitte US which is the largest professional services organization in the United States with over 170,000 professionals. Ten years ago, she was asked to lead a team that was being challenged to improve the business's operations. She went into the role feeling pressure that everyone expected her to know everything and to turn things around. For the first few months she really struggled but she didn't want to admit it to anyone because she didn't want it to appear that she wasn't the right person for the job. In fact, she handled most things from behind her computer because it was easier for her to sit in her office and fire off emails tackling her to-do list than to invest the time to get to know her team and bring them along on the journey.

Not being able to achieve my desired outcomes and live up to my expectations of myself—and the expectations that others had of me—really made me question who I was as a leader and whether I was the right person for the job. I went to my direct supervisor who put me in that role and I told him, "I don't think I'm the right person for this role today and I can't make the changes that you want me to make." He said, "I have confidence in you and you're the right person for the role. I knew you didn't have all the skills needed. Part of why I chose you was because I wanted a fresh perspective. Someone in this role who has 'been there and done that' wouldn't be the right fit." When he told me this, I really went on a journey and began talking to people about my capabilities. I had been a very "command-and-control" leader, and I realized that I was upsetting those around me. I was so results-driven and focused on the short term that I wasn't thinking about the human element or how it made people feel. I went on a real journey and reflected on what kind of leader and person I wanted to be. I met with people and told them that I wasn't doing my job well and gave them space to acknowledge that. It was a very vulnerable feeling.

Lara was confronted with the most difficult question leaders can ask of themselves, "Who am I as a leader?" This is a tough and deep question to explore but it is necessary because it forces you to seek answers and solutions.

When looking at these four types of questions for leaders, remember a few things:

- They are not mutually exclusive. For example, you can feel vulnerability in more than one part of your body and you can ask more than one question at the same time.

- This isn't a vulnerability scale with the exception of questioning the soul, which is always what makes leaders feel most vulnerable.

- Mind, body, and heart can lead to soul vulnerability. For example, you can share an idea that receives negative feedback, which then makes you question who you are as a leader and as a person.

These are all natural questions for us to ask in our personal and professional lives. I go through a variety of these questions every single day after interactions with friends, team meetings, emails I send out, or conversations I have with friends and family.

Sometimes these questions will make you feel uncomfortable and vulnerable and other times they will just pop in as surface-level things to think about. As a leader, when you are feeling vulnerable, it can be helpful to take a step back and ask why. Which one of these questions are you asking yourself and how is that making you feel?

Many of us get stuck when we dwell and ruminate. When the question keeps circling around in our minds and it doesn't seem to go away.

Here are some things you can do to get clarity:

- Identify which one of the questions you are seeking to answer and, if you can, why this question came up in your mind.
- We feel stress in our bodies. Check in with those parts of your body that you feel stress if something is off, like your throat, stomach, and so on.
- If something feels wrong in your gut, it probably is. Listen to your instinctual reaction.
- If a decision or action you're making or taking is not in line with your values, it probably will come up in your body. When we are living our purpose, there is less friction, and our spirit feels light.
- Confide in someone you trust to see if you can get some more perspective or insights.

It is clear that although the factors that make us feel vulnerable can vary, our ability to be vulnerable is closely tied to the leadership and culture of the team or organization. Although vulnerability is an inevitable aspect of human nature, we have the power to choose whether or not to openly express it and lead with vulnerability.

IV

What Happens to Leaders When They Are Vulnerable?

17

Getting Past the Defense!

I present you with two urns, each containing 100 balls.

Urn A has an even mix of 50 black and 50 red balls. Urn B has an unknown mix of red and black balls.

Knowing this, which one of the following scenarios would you select?

A: Get $100 if red is drawn from urn A, or else get nothing.
B: Get $100 if black is drawn from urn A, or else get nothing.
C: Get $100 if red is drawn from urn B, or else get nothing.
D: Get $100 is black is drawn from urn B, or else get nothing.

When doing this experiment, participants don't show a preference between options A and B, which makes sense because the odds are the same, 50%.

However, most participants prefer A to C and B to D. In options A and B we again know that the odds are 50%, but in C and D we have no idea what the probabilities of outcomes are, so we avoid them.

Humans don't like uncertainty and we prefer outcomes and situations with low uncertainty over those where the uncertainty is higher even if those highly uncertain outcomes have a higher reward. Think about this in the context of vulnerability, which is a very uncertain feeling. It's not our default mode to be in. We try to avoid it even if there's a higher reward involved.

When we feel vulnerable, the immediate physiological reaction is that our body warns us of any potential threats, something we refer to as fight-or-flight. Many years ago, this would help us from getting eaten by lions. In organizations today, this manifests in emotional instead of physical vulnerability, although the feeling we get feels the same. Whether you're being chased by a lion or have to talk about a mistake you made in front of your peers, the reactions we get are similar.

Colin Camerer is a behavioral economist at the California Institute of Technology, where he teaches classes on behavior, decision-making, and game theory. He is one of the world's leading experts in a field known as neuroeconomics, which blends economics and neuroscience to study our habits of decision-making. It strives to answer the question of why we make decisions the way we do.

Colin did some early fMRI experiments based on the urn example, and he discovered something very interesting. There's an old evolutionary part of our brains called the amygdala, which activates when it perceives a threat. In an experiment, Colin and his team showed participants a neutral face and while they are looking at it they quickly flicker in a fearful face. It's done so rapidly that participants don't even consciously know that they saw it, but the amygdala does. The amygdala is what gives humans, in part, our flight-or-fight response. That's been pretty invaluable for keeping us around for tens of thousands of years! Colin explains it's like a guard dog in your house that barks when it senses danger. It doesn't know what that danger is but it still barks. The amygdala is a very primitive warning system and when you are not sure what the odds are in a situation, for example, sharing a mistake with a team member, asking for help, or showing emotion, you get this very quick fear signal spike and your brain starts thinking "maybe things are going against me." Uncertainty triggers fear.

As a result, our defenses go up. When you're in fight-or-flight your heart beats faster to give your body more energy and oxygen for a rapid response, your pupils dilate so that you can be more attuned to your surroundings, your skin becomes pale as blood is redirected to vital organs, and your muscles tremble as you get ready for action.

At work you aren't going to physically fight anyone nor are you going to sprint out of the building never to be seen again. Although you might get that fight-or-flight feeling, your emotional vulnerability defenses are going to include a different arsenal.

I don't like being vulnerable and my mind, body, heart, and soul all know it, and yours does, too. When I'm put in vulnerable situations, my body goes into defense mode, and I have to say, I'm pretty damn good at defending. I have three techniques I use and perhaps you have used them as well. The first is stonewalling, which is exactly what it sounds like. Whenever I feel vulnerable I turn into a rock, my emotions shut down, and my brain comes out swinging with all sorts of logical answers and responses to whatever the discussion might be about.

The second defensive resource I use is humor. I will take a serious situation and try to turn it into something less serious by either smiling or laughing or maybe even making some kind of a funny sarcastic comment. By doing so, I deflect the vulnerability and turn it into something funny.

My third defense mechanism is to be critical. I'm very quick to point out flaws and issues with something or someone when I'm feeling vulnerable. This is something that Barbara Humpton from Siemens has experienced as well: "A defense mechanism I've discovered, and that I've worked to fix, is an internal discussion I have with myself when I ask 'Who's fault is this?' It's a natural human reaction when facing a problem to look for all kinds of ways to rationalize why I'm right and why someone else is to blame, but it's not healthy or helpful. Now that I'm conscious of this reaction and instinct, I can rein it in and redirect it in a way that's more productive. I can instead put my energy into looking for solutions."

I can relate to Barbara's experiences. When I'm feeling vulnerable, I know exactly what I'm doing when my defenses go up and I just can't stop these things from happening. There are lots of defensive mechanisms you might deploy, but the point is to be aware of them.

I've learned that the best way to get around my defenses is to give myself some time and space. For example, if my wife tells me I did something to hurt her feelings or if a friend gets mad at me for something, I can't immediately dive into things because my defenses have come up. I need a few minutes to process, to identify what's going on and how I and the other person are feeling, and then I can come to the conversation or situation and be open and vulnerable about it. In fact, several times people have asked me, "Don't you have anything to say about what happened?" I do; I just need some time before I can say it and I communicate that to the other person.

The best thing you can do when you're feeling vulnerable is to pay attention to the defense mechanisms you have going up. Sometimes they go up for a good reason and can help you from getting emotionally or physically hurt. But many times, it will serve you well to get past the defenses and let the vulnerability come through.

Being a vulnerable leader isn't comfortable and it's not a default state for most of us to be in, which is why our defenses go up.

18

Critical Moments

In chess there is a concept known as critical moments, which are positions in the game that can lead to either negative or positive turning points. It's important to be able to spot critical moments and to take extra time and care before playing the next move.

This same concept applies to leadership and vulnerability. Every leader will be faced with critical moments from a strategic business perspective, but in this case, specifically, when it comes to vulnerability.

In my research for this book, I discovered that leaders feel negative emotions and sensations when they are anticipating being vulnerable and even going through the act of being vulnerable. This can include preparing to have a difficult conversation, knowing you have to admit to a mistake or failure, or sharing something personal that is affecting your performance at work. It's an uncomfortable feeling associated with negative emotions.

When I asked CEOs about situations when they felt most vulnerable, I noticed something fascinating. There was always a fork in the road that led to three different outcomes: a break-through moment, a learning moment, or a fixed moment (see Figure 18.1).

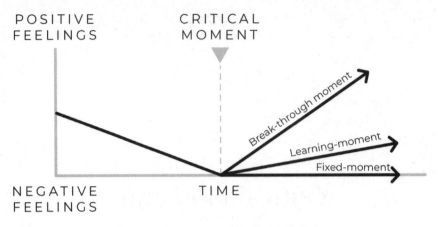

Figure 18.1 Three Outcomes of Vulnerability

Break-Through Moment

We all go through difficult and stressful situations whether it is getting surgery, proposing to someone, asking for a raise at work, or confiding in someone. Leading up to those moments and being in those moments is very vulnerable and can be stressful and anxiety inducing.

When the surgery is over, you feel relieved; when the person you proposed to says "yes," you feel ecstatic; when you get the raise at work, you feel proud and accomplished; and when you confide in someone, you feel hopeful.

A break-through moment occurs when those negative feelings and emotions turn positive. Everyone has a different vulnerability break-through point, a period when they have to get through the turbulence before they reach the calm, but that point almost always happens. There are two types of break-through moments: internal and external. The first depends on you, and the second, far more common way, depends on those around you.

Internal Break-Through Moments

To be able to create your own break-through moment, you as a leader must be fully aware of your personal values, take actions that align with those values, and then reflect on those actions and make the connection between the two. In other words, you have to realize that you did something or acted in a way that reflects what you believe in and what you stand for. Even if the intended outcome isn't reached, you can say that you were true to yourself. It's this connection between values and actions that is so important.

James Formby is the former CEO of Rand Merchant Bank in South Africa, which has more than 3,500 employees. He shared the following with me about achieving his own break-through moments: "When I'm vulnerable I feel nervous and uncertain of how others might receive my vulnerability or perceive me. However, once I say or do what needs to be done, I feel relieved and proud that I have been true to myself and open with where I am or what I'm feeling."

James's example is not common, and I can only assume it's because most leaders do not spend enough time self-reflecting on their behaviors and connecting them to their personal values.

Knowing what you stand for and what you believe in is a powerful guide that will help you determine when to be vulnerable and when to not be. When to speak up and when to stay quiet. When to confide in someone and when not to. And, most important, it will help you reach break-through points.

Tina Freese Decker is the president and CEO of Corewell Health, a nonprofit organization with more than 60,000 team members. She echoed this sentiment: "You have to know who you are, what your values are, and what you stand for. Why are you doing what you're doing? If you don't know these things, then you are just floating around. If you have a good understanding of these things and what defines you, then this will really help you to become a vulnerable leader. The best leaders are authentic, genuine, and are comfortable being themselves. They are vulnerable precisely because they know who they are and what their values are. It all starts there."

What is your North Star?

Mine is to create organizations around the world where we all want to show up to work each day and to cultivate leaders we want to work with. My passion and mission is to create great leaders, engaged employees, and future-ready organizations. I believe doing this can change the world and enable us to conquer any challenge and unlock new and amazing opportunities.

When your North Star is aligned with what your organization does, then you really have something special.

Patrick Decker is the president and CEO of Xylem, a 17,000-person water company. Patrick is one of those rare CEOs who believes in making the world a better place and positively affecting the lives of everyone his company touches:

Solving the world's biggest water challenges is my North Star. It gives me and my team purpose and direction. Without it we would be rudderless. But being purpose driven requires vulnerability. Many leaders are great at executing and delivering on their operational metrics, which is critical, but there is no vulnerability in that. What about the responsibility for the broader organization they lead and the impact they have? Instead of being solely driven by our fiduciary responsibility, I always ask, how do I keep my colleagues, customers, and communities engaged in something larger than themselves? It requires vulnerability to say I care more about our purpose than anything else.

A crucial point to remember here is that corporate and personal values themselves are just words. Whenever I speak at conferences around the world, I ask someone in the audience to share some of their personal or corporate values. They say things like "trust, transparency, having fun," and the like. I then ask everyone else in the room how many of them have one of those same values; almost everyone's hand goes up. Your values are not unique, but how you make those values come to life is.

As Bob Chapman, the CEO of Barry-Wehmiller told me, "Putting values on the wall might decorate the wall, but it doesn't translate into behaviors."

External Break-Through Moments

The second more common and perhaps even more impactful way to reach a break-through moment has very little to do with leaders themselves and everything to do with the other person or people. The secret is all about positive feedback and response. This is why people on the receiving end of vulnerability have such tremendous power and responsibility: because they can help others get to their vulnerability break-through point.

"My heart rate goes up and I get into fight-or-flight mode but it's quite fleeting for me if I sense that I'm getting connection or positive feedback. When that happens then the feeling turns to relief, comfort, calm, and hope," Iain Williamson, CEO of Old Mutual, told me.

A CEO of a large technology company shared a story with me about how he had to get on stage in front of thousands of people to give a presentation, and sitting in the front row were some of his technology and business mentors: people who started and ran companies such as Apple, Microsoft, and Cisco. He felt very vulnerable and he was freaking out. In just a few moments he was going to be thrown onto the stage and there was nothing he could do about it. As someone who has been speaking for 15 years, I know exactly what that feels like.

He walked onto the stage and started talking. His heart was beating, he was speaking quickly with a slight quiver, his body was tense, and he was in complete fight-or-flight mode. He looked at the front row where his mentors were sitting and some of them smiled at him, gave him a little air fist-bump, and nodded their heads as if to say, "You're doing a great job, you got this!" *Boom!* Break-through point reached.

That positive feedback and response helped him calm down and feel more confident. His heartbeat slowed down, he was able to speak with more confidence, and he seemed more relaxed. Without even saying a word, his mentors in the front row gave him the positive feedback he needed.

These types of break-through moments can happen in a matter of seconds, minutes, or in some cases when the positive response or feedback is delayed, a few days, weeks, or longer. You can't always control how you respond to them. When you receive positive feedback or response your feelings change without you consciously doing anything.

The ideal scenario would be when you combine both types together. You realize you acted in a way that aligns with your values and you also get the positive external response or feedback.

If something tragic happens, such as losing your job, I don't want to imply that some kind words from a coworker are going to make your problems go away, but you will certainly get a boost of those positive feelings and you will feel better.

I don't have physiological data to tell you how long this takes to happen, why it happens, or even how it happens. All I can tell you is that it has happened to everyone I've interviewed, and I bet it has happened to you as well.

Learning Moment

What happens when the break-through point isn't reached? For example, let's say you confide in someone who uses the information to insult you, make you feel small, or as a way to hurt you or your career? It's clear why the person on the receiving end of your vulnerability has so much power and responsibility. They can either help you get to your break-through point or they can torture you.

When this happens, the break-through point becomes a learning moment, if you let it. A learning moment is the point at which you acknowledge that things didn't go the right way for you, and you have to take stock of what you learned about yourself, the situation, and the other person. Acknowledging and actually telling yourself "This is a learning moment" will help those negative feelings and emotions turn positive. It's a much longer process that can take days, weeks, or longer as you reflect back on everything and ask yourself, "What did I learn and how can I apply what I learned in my career and life?"

Even though learning moments can sometimes be painful they also are powerful vehicles for growth. Leaders must never stop learning, and one CEO who understands this is Rich Bielen, the president and CEO of Protective Life Corporation, an almost 4,000-person insurance, annuity, and asset protection company: "A few years ago, I was doing an end-of-year presentation for a group of interns. Someone in the back row raised their hand and asked, 'When do you think you've learned it all?' I looked at them and said, 'If you ever "learn it all," it's all over for you because it means the world has passed you by. Leaders must always be learning. The world is always changing, and you are always building new relationships and connections with other human beings.'"

These learning moments don't always have to revolve around negative things although they typically do. They can also be positive. For example, genuinely recognizing people and showing appreciation can be a vulnerable experience, but if you see that it connects with people in a positive way, then that learning moment will be how you recognize people in future situations.

Learning moments are conscious moments that you control. You have the power and the choice to say to yourself, "This is a learning moment. What did I learn and what will I do as a result now and in the future?"

One CEO of a 20,000-person European telecommunications company who wanted to remain anonymous shared a painful story with me of how she was vulnerable and it was used against her:

I've always believed in being myself. My career mantra has always been be honest with yourself and be honest with your leader, then you will get the best out of yourself and the relationship you have with your leader. But this was used against me in a terrible way with a smart CEO who identified my insecurities about my background, even if they weren't always expressly shown. I was an outsider in a company and even though I achieved success, I never went to a university and didn't go down the traditional path like this CEO did.

I talk about career failures, my father's death and how it still drives me today, challenges that I'm faced with, and things I want to improve. Earlier on in my career I was the CFO of a company and I noticed that gradually I was not being invited to important meetings. My office used to be next door to the CEO and after coming back from a holiday it was moved down the corridor into a much smaller space. I started to get ridiculed and made fun of for making certain business decisions. I took over IT from the CEO and IT was a huge mess, and she would tease me about it and blamed my leadership for it being a mess even though she was the one running IT before I took it over. Members of my team were being offered jobs in other parts of the company without my knowledge or input and the coach whom I was assigned I later found out was reporting everything I said back to the CEO. It was a huge mess and I lost a lot of my self-confidence. It really affected me psychologically; it was psychological bullying. The CEO then told me she wanted to put me on a performance improvement plan and I just told her I was going to leave. She knew that confidence was something I was trying to work on and she used that vulnerability against me. Unfortunately, I saw this coming because I had seen her do this to others. Work was my escape when my father passed away. Achievement has been a big part of me, and so I never spoke up because I was terrified of getting fired and failing.

Amazingly this didn't deter her from continuing to be vulnerable with her future teams and organizations. Instead, she viewed this as a pivotal learning moment in her leadership career and one of her most important leadership lessons:

This was a powerful learning moment for me. I learned that as you go into new environments, teams, and organizations, you have to really understand who you are going to be working with. You have to understand the values of the people you are going to be working with, the values of the company, and the culture that exists. Do your due diligence. I realized that I only want to align myself with people and companies that have a purpose, values, and culture that align with my approach to life, which is to be open, honest, transparent, and willing to be vulnerable.

From the survey data, 73% of leaders said that they have been vulnerable at work and had it backfire at least once in their careers. In fact, I can almost guarantee that being vulnerable at work will backfire at some point in your career. It's not a common regular occurrence but it will happen.

Nothing in life is a guarantee so why should vulnerability be any different? Being vulnerable is an act of trust. It doesn't mean you will never be betrayed, but it won't happen nearly as often as you think. As we can learn from this CEO, if vulnerability is ever used against you, it's a sign you shouldn't be working for that team or leader to begin with. This leader consciously turned a very negative experience into a very powerful learning moment that eventually helped her become CEO.

Guy Meldrum, president and CEO of Reynolds American Inc. with almost 4,000 employees, leads with learning moments: "You're not perfect and you're not going to get vulnerability right every time. You have to recognize employees have their own opinions, and as a leader you need to respect them. When things don't go the right way you have a choice: you can let those situations cripple you or you can learn from them. When you focus on learning moments, you give yourself permission to keep being vulnerable and create a safe environment for those around you to do the same."

Fixed Moment

This is a dangerous place to be in and should be avoided at all costs. These fixed moments are what prevent leaders from growing or evolving. This is what turns people into "stereotypical leaders."

A fixed moment occurs when a leader acknowledges that being vulnerable didn't go according to plan and, in fact, led to negative outcomes. When this happens, the leader says things to himself such as, "I knew this was going to happen; I'm never going to be vulnerable again."

In other words, what happens is that the leader is fixing himself in a negative place that prevents him from being vulnerable in the future. You end up feeling bitter, resentful, and distrustful of the people you work with, which can be damaging to your career and those around you. A fixed moment can be a learning moment when it's situational; for example, if you are vulnerable with someone, it doesn't go well, and you realize you shouldn't be vulnerable with that person again. It's a learning moment because it's situational and not a personal attribute. There's a difference between saying "I am not a vulnerable person" versus "I'm no longer going to be vulnerable with John." The first example is a definition of who you are as a leader and person, whereas the second one is something you are applying to a situation.

Jeff Dailey is the president and CEO of Farmers Insurance, a 21,000-person company. Jeff understands the difference between a fixed and learning moment: "Confidence gets shattered when a leader is vulnerable and it doesn't go as planned. For example, sharing a mistake that is met with criticism. The real danger happens when leaders don't use these as learning moments but instead use these as reasons for why they should never be vulnerable again. They are fixed in a negative and fear-based way of thinking. If you're afraid to share any challenge, mistake, or struggle, then you just close down and hide from everything. That's not leadership."

Once you get into a fixed moment, it can be difficult to get out of it as you generally become distrustful of those around you and you don't allow for the optimistic correction that I talked about previously. The only way out of a fixed moment is—you guessed it—to be vulnerable again and give yourself the opportunity to go through either a break-through moment or a learning moment.

Fixed and learning moments are conscious moments. You can decide if you want to learn from the experience or if you want to use the experience as a way to cement yourself in your current way of thinking and behaving. You can see how this all plays out in Figure 18.2. When you feel vulnerable at work, if you share

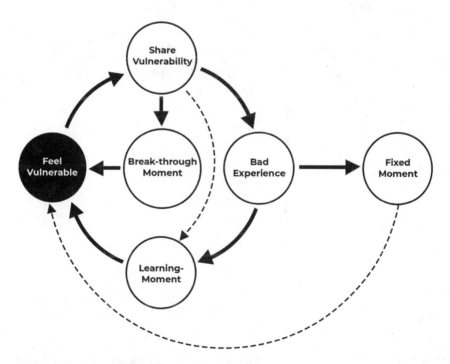

Figure 18.2 The vulnerability loop

your vulnerability (when appropriate), you get either a break-through moment with a positive response or a bad experience, in which case you can choose to view that as a learning moment and then go back to embracing vulnerability. Or, you can let that negative experience create a fixed moment for you, which locks you in a negative way of thinking. The only way out of that is to go back to the starting point.

It's essential to understand these three moments, because when you're vulnerable you can make sure that you always have a positive outcome, even if that outcome isn't immediate.

Learning moments help create other learning moments, and fixed moments help create other fixed moments, which is why it's easy to fall into a negative fixed loop. However, the flipside is also true. If you can teach yourself to focus on learning moments, then you will be stuck in a positive learning loop. The good news is that even with break-through moments, which you can't always control, you can still learn from them and they still help you learn and grow as a leader.

When you recognize that the worst-case scenario from being vulnerable is that you will have a learning moment, then you realize how valuable leading with vulnerability can be. The more learning moments you have the more you grow and develop. Learning moments help you become an even stronger superhero and a better version of yourself.

19

What Does Vulnerability Feel Like?

Dr. Love, aka Paul Zak, is a professor of economic sciences, psychology, and management director at the Center for Neuroeconomics Studies at Claremont Graduate University. He has been studying vulnerability, empathy, and trustworthiness on a scientific level for a long time. He looks not just at the emotional responses but also at the chemical responses in our brains and bodies via extensive blood testing.

It turns out then when we are vulnerable, it produces a stress response via the release of adrenaline and cortisol, making us uncomfortable, something clearly reflected in some of the following responses. We've all been there, right?

We can all experience vulnerability in different ways, but every CEO told me vulnerability always manifests in some physical way. One of the questions I asked more than 100 CEOs was "When you're vulnerable, what does that feel like in your body?" Here are some of the responses I got back.

"Vulnerability is something I deal with regularly. It brings me back to being the 10-year-old kid, called on by the teacher in front of the class to recite the poem he 'forgot' to learn, as it triggers a wave of cold sweat and unleashes the guilt of not being good enough. Courage is the remedy!"

—Aart de Geus, CEO, Synopsys

185

"Vulnerability feels like being apprehensive and even frightened about something to feeling hopeless or being angered. It's not a feeling that generates happiness, and it's one that I'd prefer not to have."

—Curt Morgan, former president and CEO,
Vistra Corporation

"My heart is racing, I can't articulate my words properly, and when I speak in almost a quivering kind of way because I'm nervous."

—Sal Abbate, CEO, Veritiv

"It can feel uncomfortable, both emotionally and physically. I sometimes feel like I am losing my balance and grounding. The day I understood I feel what I think—that day changed my life. This simple understanding of how the mind and emotions work has helped me get through difficult situations."

—Ilham Kadri, CEO, Solvay

"I can feel that I'm in fight-or-flight mode, my heart beats faster, and my stomach is in knots. It almost feels like a panic attack, which I have had a few times.

—CEO, agriculture company

None of the CEOs I interviewed said, "Leading with vulnerability feels great. I love it!" That stress response is hard at work. If it's always super-uncomfortable and stressful to ask for help or to admit you're having a bad day, then why do it? Think about all of the times you have achieved a goal. How many of those times did you have to push yourself? Probably all of them. Growth doesn't come from being comfortable. As a leader it's your responsibility and privilege to force yourself outside of your comfort zone to be able to connect with others and unlock the potential of those around you. This is what you signed up for. Vulnerability isn't supposed to be comfortable, but growth never is. Remember what Frank Blake, the former CEO of The Home Depot said. Being a leader means that you give a piece of yourself to your people. If you aren't prepared for that, then don't strive for a leadership position.

The good news is the more vulnerable and open you become, the less the stress response makes itself present. However, people on the receiving end of our vulnerability see this as a sign of trust and their brains get a dose of oxytocin, which causes three things to happen.

First, it causes a reduction in physiological stress, meaning people become more comfortable around you because you let your guard down. This is crucial especially in leadership when we need people to be comfortable around leaders to share ideas, opportunities, struggles, and to have tough and uncomfortable conversations.

Second, the dose of oxytocin increases empathy in people, which allows them to become more physiologically connected to you. One of my big character flaws is my tendency to be critical. At a recent family gathering I told Blake that she needs to be less controlling with our son, Noah. I made this comment in front of family members, which naturally upset her and caused us to get into an argument later that evening. Whenever my wife and I argue about something, my default mode is to turn into a giant block of ice. I don't talk and I just shut Blake out, which makes her more upset and frustrated.

If Blake is visibly upset with me and tells me that I hurt her feelings, my impenetrable ice shield melts. I'm sure you have experienced something like this in your life as well. When we are vulnerable it allows people to connect with us. It's just biologically how we are wired.

The third result of that hit of oxytocin is that it creates a desire for the other person to put in effort to help you even if this means they can't help you directly. Let's say you are working on a proposal for a client but you need help with the marketing side of things. If you approach one of your experienced peers and say, "Hey, I'd love your help with some marketing ideas for this new prospect I'm trying to pitch. I'm really struggling. Do you have an hour or two that you can spare?" then when they get their dose of oxytocin they will have a desire to help you. However, even if they can't help you directly, they may respond with, "I'd love to help you but I'm completely swamped. But I know that

Jeanenne on my team is really good at that stuff and she should have some time to spend with you." Meaning, if they can't help you directly, they can connect you with someone who can help you.[1]

A word of caution for all of you out there who are thinking, "Great, I can just fake my way to connection." Well, bad news for you: you can't. According to Dr. Zak, when you fake vulnerability we can tell, not always on a conscious level, but on a subconscious level. It turns out that our brains are pretty amazing bullsh*t indicators. To make matters even worse, when people try to fake vulnerability, they actually get a negative physiological response via the release of epinephrine. The faker is afraid of being found out. The only time this negative response doesn't happen is if the person is a sociopath.

Dr. James Downing is the president and CEO of St. Jude Children's Research Hospital, an organization with more than 6,000 employees. Here's what he shared with me: "Vulnerability for a leader is essential. Leaders who aren't honest with themselves and don't present honest personas can't lead as effectively. People will see when you're faking, and they won't follow. It's important for leaders to recognize their strengths and weaknesses, acknowledge areas for improvement, and work to better their skills. Most important, be honest with yourself, and then be honest with the people you lead."

Dr. Zak also told me that there are a few situations in which vulnerability doesn't really work. The first is when there are very high levels of stress. For example, you're in a tough meeting and you want to make it through the next 10 minutes and get out of there. In these moments, we don't rely on our social resources. Another situation is when there are high levels of testosterone present. For example, 15-year-old males aren't thinking about other people; they want to compete against them and beat them in anything and everything. Young males are not thinking or focusing on vulnerability and teamwork. As we get into our 30s when many of us have kids and committed relationships, our levels of testosterone go down. In organizations that are highly competitive and where testosterone levels are high, the culture becomes about beating those around you as opposed to focusing on teamwork or trust. This means that the cultural environment plays an important role in vulnerability at work and in leadership. This is why Dr. Zak says one of the best things we can do is to critique in private and praise in public.

You might be wondering how all of this translates into the virtual world now that hybrid work is the new reality. According to Dr. Zak, we get 50% to 80% of the oxytocin dose in online environments compared to when we are vulnerable in-person. Clearly there is still value for in-person connection and interaction.

Why do our perceptions of vulnerability change depending on if we are thinking about ourselves or others? Imagine you have a meeting with your team and admit that you don't know how to do something or that you made a mistake on a project. How would that make you feel?

Now imagine that someone else on your team was in your position, and they were the one admitting they made a mistake or didn't know how to do something. How do you perceive them?

Anna Bruk, Sabine G. Scholl, and Herbert Bless of the University of Mannheim in Germany published a study in 2018 called "Beautiful Mess Effect: Self–Other Differences in Evaluation of Showing Vulnerability."[2] Researchers asked participants to imagine themselves in a variety of vulnerable situations, including admitting to making a crucial mistake at work or being the first to apologize to a romantic partner after a big fight. The fascinating thing is that when people imagined themselves in these situations they perceived themselves as being rather weak or inadequate, which in the survey data in "Beautiful Mess Effect" is the number-one reason that keeps us from being vulnerable at work. However, when they imagined other people being vulnerable in these situations; they perceived them as being relatively "strong" and "courageous."

This can be explained by a theory in social psychology called construal level theory, which describes how psychological distance determines if we think about something in an abstract or concrete way. For instance, if you look at a tree close up, you'll see all the details—the branches, the leaves, and the trunk. But from a mile away, you'll only see a general silhouette.

Distance also can take several forms, such as temporal (the distance between now and a decade later) and social (the distance between oneself and another person). In the context of vulnerability, the social distance is crucial to understand and can influence our perceptions. When you think about yourself, the social distance is small, and the things you think about are concrete. When you think about someone else, the social distance is much greater and therefore the things you think about are more abstract.

The fascinating thing is that when we have low levels of distance, such as thinking about ourselves, we tend to think about things that are more negative and practical, but when we have high levels of distance, we think about things that are more positive and desirable.

According to Dr. Bruk and her colleagues, when we imagine someone else being vulnerable we are socially distant so we tend to think of more abstract and favorable things, such as "that person was brave for sharing that" or "asking for help is a sign of strength," but when we think of ourselves in vulnerable situations we are not socially distant, and therefore we think in more concrete ways and we imagine every flaw that people will see and every possible way that the interaction can go wrong. We tend to say things to ourselves like "people will perceive me as being incompetent if I ask for help" or "I will be rejected if I share anything personal about myself."[3]

Ironically, when we observe a physical object up close, we get more clarity, depth, and information about it. But when we emotionally observe ourselves up close the picture is fuzzy, shallow, and the information is inaccurate because we exaggerate the negative things while ignoring the positive. How do we get a clearer picture and deal with stress and negative emotions that might arise from self-examination and exploration?

As Dr. Bruk and her colleagues mentioned, when we have distance our perception tends to be more favorable so the answer is that you create distance.

Thousands of years ago King Solomon ruled the land of Israel. He was considered a wise man and people from afar would come to him to seek his counsel and advice. His insights and judgment were the best in the land. However, when it came to his own life, it was filled with problems. He was obsessed with self-indulgence and flaunting his wealth, had over 1,000 wives and concubines, and was not able to properly raise his own son to be heir to the throne.

How is it that some leaders are so great at being objective and giving other people advice and guidance, yet they struggle when it comes to their own lives? We all struggle with this, especially leaders, because we are so immersed in a situation and experience. This is known as Solomon's paradox.

Another researcher and psychologist I had the privilege of speaking with is Ethan Kross, who wrote the best-selling book, *Chatter: The Voice in Our Head, Why It Matters, and How to Harness It*. He discovered something fascinating about how we talk to ourselves, which is very much related to what Dr. Bruk and her colleagues discovered about vulnerability.

When people become stressed or emotionally uncomfortable, they tend to zoom in on their problems, like a scientist with a microscope who's trying to spot every detail. We get tunnel vision to the point where the only thing we can see are problems and challenges. To help manage this and get more emotional control, stability, and promote wise thinking, Dr. Kross discovered that a crucial skill is being able to create distance. There's no single way to distance yourself. For example, meditation can be a useful tool for distancing because you try to separate yourself from your thoughts. You might imagine your thoughts as clouds in the sky that are drifting around or disappearing or perhaps you might see your thoughts as different types of children playing in a field. This practice helps you create distance and it's one of the reasons why I started meditating for 10 minutes every morning. Meditation enables me to take a step back and see things in context as opposed to how I'm feeling or thinking at that moment. As a result, I'm able to talk to myself as I'm talking to a good friend, with compassion and positivity.

A very useful and practical tool to create distance is to use your name in a situation. Years ago I gave a talk for a large telecommunications company. I thought I did a pretty good job. People laughed at my jokes and I received some great questions and compliments. A few days later I received an email from one of the leaders at the company telling me how disappointed they were in my presentation. They thought I didn't spend enough time customizing the talk, understanding their business, or focusing on the people in the room. Immediately my internal chatter started. "I gave a talk to this great company and I totally screwed it up. How could I do something so stupid and why was I so lazy? Maybe I should just stop this whole speaking thing."

But what happens if I had changed *I* to my name? I should have said, "Jacob gave a talk to a telecommunications company and he thought he did a good job but received some tough feedback. Jacob shouldn't beat himself up. We all make mistakes, and even though he was upset he learned an important lesson from that experience that he can bring to all future speaking engagements."

I was so immersed in the situation and the experience that I couldn't see clearly and I just kept beating myself up. But had I approached it as if I was talking to my friend Jacob, my advice would have been more compassionate, objective, and helpful.

According to Ethan, when we use our own names to advise ourselves and think through a problem, we turn on our mental machine of thinking about other people; we change our perspective. In other words, we create distance. However, as

Ethan cautioned me when we spoke, this tool enables you to give yourself the best advice you're capable of giving, but this doesn't mean that advice is always going to default to "be vulnerable," and in some cases the advice you give yourself may be, "don't be vulnerable." Creating distance is also not meant as a guise for avoidance. There's a fine line between trying to ignore and not acknowledge emotions or reflecting on them without getting sucked into the vortex of negativity.

Similarly, if you are basking in praise you receive for being such a great and amazing leader, do you want to create distance? No, you want to stay immersed and present in that situation. To perpetuate that positive response, you want to avoid distance. There are times, though, when even in positive situations you want to create distance to get control over your emotions, for example, if you're laughing at a funeral or cheering that one of your peers got fired.

When it comes to being a vulnerable leader there will be many situations when you will need to fight that self-doubt and negativity and also identify when you shouldn't be vulnerable.

Before COVID, I played in a weekly chess tournament in San Francisco. I was doing well in my group and one day I showed up to my weekly game to play against an opponent who was rated about 1600, which is relatively strong for amateur players like me. We played for about six hours and ultimately I ended up losing the game. I reviewed the game with my coach afterwards and he said, "You were completely winning. Why didn't you just push your pawn down the board and promote to a queen?" I didn't have a good response. During the game I imagined all sorts of threats by my opponent, which were actually not threats at all. One of the things chess players struggle with is this concept of "seeing ghosts," that is, seeing threats that aren't really there. We get so into our own thoughts that we convince ourselves that something bad is going to happen, when in reality our position is completely fine and in fact we are winning. Being vulnerable is the same thing. Most of us aren't vulnerable because we see ghosts; we see a threat that isn't really there and it keeps us from achieving our goals and connecting with other human beings.

Jack Roche is the president and CEO of The Hanover Insurance Group, which has more than 4,400 employees. He's seen his fair share of ghosts during his leadership journey.

> I'm sensitive to what people are thinking about me or seeing in my behavior. Sometimes this happens to the point where I see things that aren't even there. I'm anticipating and imagining some kind of verbal or nonverbal exchange, and when that happens I often have to pause and actually inquire with the other person or team to make sure I'm understanding something in the right way. I try to ask more questions and clarify things without making assumptions. Leaders are never as good as we think we are at listening and understanding others' perspectives, which is why we need to ask questions and be honest with ourselves and let other people be honest with us.

Of course, sometimes the ghosts turn out to be real, meaning the threat is actually there and you can end up losing the game, or in non-chess speak, sometimes people can actually hurt you, stab you in the back, or use your vulnerability against you. We take a risk when we go outside, when we ask someone out on a date, when we ask for a promotion or more money, or when we admit to mistakes. Just because we get hurt shouldn't keep us from moving forward and trying again; otherwise, the world would be a boring and lonely place.

Levon Aronian is one of the world's top chess players. What's interesting about Aronian is that whenever he resigns a game he does so with a smile. I don't know about you, but when I lose at anything the last thing I want to do is smile. During a recent tournament a commentator asked him about this and his response was "I love the game of chess and I always remember that there is lots of suffering in life and when you are not suffering you should be grateful. If I am well enough and I am playing chess, that means I'm doing great and I appreciate that. I do get angry when I lose but never at my opponent. When my opponent beats me by playing well I can only clap and say 'Thank you for the lesson.'"[4]

We can apply the same approach in the workplace. Part of being vulnerable means putting yourself out there, making the move on the chessboard that you are uncertain about, and if it comes back to bite you, then you turn it into a learning moment.

I did an informal poll on LinkedIn in which I asked my community if they have ever been vulnerable at work and had it backfire. Over 1,000 people responded with an astounding 85% saying yes. I've also heard this quite a bit during conversations I've had with employees.

The thing you need to remember is that when people try to use your vulnerability against you, it's not a reflection of you, it's a reflection of them and the type of person they are. But sometimes, having your vulnerability used against you isn't done with malice or ill intent.

Take, for example, Alison Martin, the CEO of EMEA (Europe, Middle East, and Africa) and bank distribution for Zurich Insurance Group. The company has about 56,000 employees and Alison is responsible for more than one-third of them.

Alison is a mother to two girls whom she loves dearly, and Alison also believes in letting people into her life so her team can get to know her as a human being. She talks about her family and her kids and things that are going on outside of work.

One day earlier in her career at another company, she showed up to work to find out that someone had been promoted to a new leadership position that she would have loved to have. Alison didn't even know the position was open and she became very confused. She approached the hiring manager and said, "Why didn't you consider me for the role?" To which the hiring manager replied, "We assumed you wouldn't want the role because you have kids." Alison couldn't believe that someone else made a decision on her behalf without even talking to her about it. The hiring manager assumed that Alison wouldn't want the role because it would require more time, commitment, and energy from her, which she either wouldn't have or wouldn't want to commit to. They did it out of what they thought was the best intention, not out of malice; they didn't want Alison to try to have to pick between work and family so they did it for her.

I asked Alison if that experience made her never want to share anything personal at work again. She replied, "No, because there's not enough hours in the day for you to try and be two different people. That time is much better spent getting to know the people you work with and letting them get to know you. Nobody is perfect, so why pretend?"

We keep hearing about the importance of purpose and meaning for employees, which is something I explored in great detail in my book *The Future Leader*. But here's the thing that lots of leaders forget. Purpose and meaning don't exist without human connection, which is needed to have your people trust you. And that doesn't happen without vulnerability. When leaders frequently show a willingness to be emotionally vulnerable, their direct reports are twice as likely to find their jobs full of meaning and purpose.

V

How to Lead with Vulnerability

20

Unlocking your Superpower

Anyone can learn how to lead with vulnerability and unlock this superpower for themselves and those around them. This section of the book will give you the tools and resources to make that happen, but it's up to you to put these tools to work. You will learn about the eight attributes of vulnerable leaders, you'll discover the vulnerability wheel and how to use it to make sure that when you are vulnerable you will have the highest chance of a positive outcome, and you will begin your journey up the vulnerability mountain armed with everything you have learned so far.

Joe Almeida is the CEO of Baxter International, a health-care company with more than 60,000 employees. He knows how powerful vulnerability for leaders can be when done the right way and, as he points out, being a vulnerable leader isn't just about you; it's about the impact you have on those around you.

> I can share this with confidence because I've seen both sides. Early in my career, I worked in cultures defined by competition and hierarchy. Openness and vulnerability were readily dismissed as liabilities. Thankfully, healthier perspectives emerged as my learning continued, and key mentors confirmed that these ostensible weaknesses were actually among the greatest tools at my disposal when navigating obstacles and

delivering exceptional results. The true strength of vulnerability has revealed itself time and again throughout my leadership journey, but maybe never more than when facing a crisis or decisive turning point impacting our company and the communities we serve. Many recent examples come to mind: COVID-19 and its sustained repercussions . . . the fight for racial justice . . . war in Ukraine . . . and a string of natural disasters globally. Just one of these would be sufficient to bring the power of vulnerability to light; and, surely, no reasonable leader can pretend to have the insight to go it alone when facing a confluence of tests like these. Even so, it's far better to embrace this power before confronting such pivotal moments. Vulnerability might seem like an inward, personal trait, but it's really about empowering others to make their own mark and contribute at the highest levels.

Many CEOs I interviewed who also worked for both stereotypical and vulnerable leaders have made the same realization. Again, it is clear, you cannot lead through change without vulnerability on behalf of leaders.

There are many leaders like Joe who have made this same realization. Vulnerability for leaders can have a tremendous positive impact on those around them because it enables you and those around you to do more and to be more.

21

The Five Vulnerable Leader Superheroes

Wonder Woman can fly and has super-strength and speed. Spider-Man can shoot webs from his hands, climb walls, and has amazing reflexes. Wolverine has claws that grow from his hands, can heal himself, and has enhanced senses.

Superheroes all have their own abilities, strengths, and weaknesses. There isn't one kind of superhero just like there isn't one kind of vulnerable leader. It's important to understand this because the general assumption we have about being a vulnerable leader is that either you are or you aren't. But it's not so black-and-white; it's quite gray.

What makes up these different types of vulnerable leader superheroes isn't a defined set of rules but comfort levels that may change over time. As you read through the different superhero types, instead of asking yourself "Which one am I?" ask yourself, "Which one am I most comfortable with being?" This is because you might not see yourself as completely one type of superhero but maybe a little bit of an amalgamation, but focusing on which one you are most comfortable with will give you a much clearer picture of the superhero you are.

While interviewing more than 100 CEOs I noticed that they were all vulnerable in different ways. For example, some were more comfortable sharing personal challenges and struggles, whereas others were more comfortable talking about mistakes and failures in a work context. I identified five types of vulnerable leaders; each of them have their own unique abilities, strengths, and weaknesses.

Captain Heart

Captain Heart wears their heart on their sleeve, and they are as authentic and transparent as they get. It's not uncommon for Captain Heart to actually say, "With me, what you see is what you get." These types of leaders are comfortable sharing anything and everything with anyone. They can talk about personal challenges and struggles at work, ask for help on a crucial project, admit to a mistake, show positive and negative emotion, and try to be as much of an open book as they can. Captain Heart also doesn't set specific boundaries and barriers between work and life, and they believe in being a single authentic version of themselves at all times.

Captain Heart is able to quickly build relationships and connections with other people as a result of their openness. They are also able to thrive in a variety of complex situations ranging from tough meetings at work to casual get-togethers outside of work. Because Captain Heart is so transparent there's also not a lot of emotional baggage they have to carry around, everything is out there, and there is no ambiguity about what they believe in or where they stand on certain issues because they are never afraid to speak up. This type of vulnerable leader is considered by many to be brave and courageous. Because they are comfortable with themselves they are also self-aware.

Captain Heart is not invincible, though. Because they are so open, they are also more susceptible to attack. It's very easy to take information they share and use it against them in either a personal or professional setting. When those around you know so much about you it's not hard to see why this can be the case. This type of vulnerable leader might also make those around them feel uncomfortable because not everyone is okay with being as open and transparent. Captain Heart might also periodically get in trouble for saying the wrong thing.

Abilities

- Quickly builds relationships and connections
- Thrives in a variety of complex situations
- Nimble and agile due to carrying minimal weight on their shoulders
- Eliminates ambiguity because their emotions are clear
- Not afraid to speak up and is considered courageous and brave
- Intuitive and curious
- Charismatic
- Emotionally intelligent

Weaknesses

- More susceptible to attack
- Can feel overbearing or overwhelming to others
- Might make others feel uncomfortable
- Might get in trouble for saying the wrong thing
- Can be perceived as "too vulnerable" and an "oversharer"

This is from Sheryl Palmer, the CEO of Taylor Morrison, a 3,200-person home building company, which not coincidentally has been ranked as the number-one most trusted home builder in America for the past seven years!

I wear my heart on my sleeve but I have thick skin. I'm a sensitive and emotional person and other people can see it. Sometimes if something is really upsetting and impacting me, I have to leave the office. And if my way of dealing with something is crying, then I'd go to my car and do that. Over time I developed more self-confidence and I learned that if I'm going to show up as my authentic self, then sometimes my team is going to see that sensitive side of me, and if I'm feeling really hurt, I'm going to be honest with them and not hide it.

Wonder Worker

Wonder Worker is more comfortable being vulnerable about all things work related. This means they are comfortable saying "I don't know," asking for help, talking about work-related mistakes or failures, and giving and receiving candid feedback. They are not as comfortable sharing personal information or anything that falls outside of the context of work. It doesn't mean they never will, but it requires them really getting outside of their comfort zone to do so. Wonder Worker prefers to have more established boundaries between work and life and tends to be more private with their personal life.

This type of leader is great at connecting with people on a professional level and creating a strong culture focused on learning and growth. Because Wonder Worker has a strong focus on learning, growth, and improvement at work, they are able to create very effective and productive teams and can unlock the potential of those around them. They are also a master of boundaries.

However, if you are a Wonder Worker, your team members might feel like they don't know the "real you" because most of what you share tends to be focused on work. You might also struggle with creating very high levels of trust and belonging. Last, you might find maintaining boundaries to be a challenge over time as you constantly work to balance your personal and professional self.

Abilities

- Connects with people on a professional level
- Creates a culture of learning and growth
- A master of boundaries
- Gets the most out of people
- Builds strong and productive teams
- Great at driving results

Weaknesses

- Others might feel they don't know the "real you."
- Might not create as high levels of trust and belonging
- Can be challenging to maintain boundaries
- Might not get or give emotional support at work

Stephen Smith is the CEO of Amsted Industries, a global manufacturing company with more than 18,000 employees. He is one of the many Wonder Worker superheroes.

> I'm not as good at sharing things about my personal life as I should be because I'm a private person by nature. But I do understand that sharing some things are insights into your own life and that these are really valuable in the organization. I just had my second grandchild and I'm around the office showing pictures on my phone to people who normally wouldn't even expect to interact with me. I want my team to know that I'm a human being like they are and I get joy out of the same kinds of things that they do and I feel the same emotions. I'm also not shy about telling people that I'm a big White Sox fan, which isn't very common in Chicago! I try to be more open and share about my life in a way with which I am comfortable.

Professor Personal

Professor Personal is more comfortable being vulnerable about things outside of work. They are liked by many because they are more comfortable talking about aspects of themselves such as personal challenges and struggles, life outside of work, and giving insight into who they are as a person. As with Wonder Worker, it doesn't mean Professor Personal won't ever share things about work, but it's not what they are most comfortable with.

Professor Personal is great at developing strong personal connections and relationships and oftentimes has quite a few friends at work. They give insight into who they are as a person and what they care about and value. This type of vulnerable leader also creates a positive work environment where people feel more comfortable being themselves. As a result, the culture has high levels of engagement.

Although Professor Personal creates a positive culture where people feel like they belong, this superhero might struggle more often with imposter syndrome. They might also hinder their own (and their teams') professional development.

Abilities

- Develops strong personal connections and relationships
- Gives people deep insight into who they are as a person
- Creates a friendly and positive work environment where people can be their authentic selves
- Creates high levels of engagement
- Emotionally intelligent

Weaknesses

- Might not always unlock the full professional potential of people
- Might not help surface the best ideas and opportunities on a team
- Might cause team professional development to be stalled
- Imposter syndrome

One CEO of a 16,000-person education company told me,

I'm definitely more comfortable sharing things about my personal life with my team. It has helped me create some very close relationships and a culture where employees want to show up each day. I do talk about vulnerability in the context of work when I need to but it's not in my comfort zone. Throughout my career I was never encouraged to talk about life outside of work and in fact I was explicitly told that I shouldn't. However, now I see the value in doing that and my people know what I care about, what I stand for, what I believe in, and what a meaningful life looks like to me.

Super-Situational

Super-Situational adapts and blends with their environment and surroundings. They might meet with a member of their team and share that they are going through a tough time at work but then they might meet with a peer shortly after and talk about a big mistake they made on a client project. Super-Situational has very high levels of self-awareness and is good at knowing how they affect a person or a situation depending on what they are sharing. They are also capable of adapting to any situation and have a unique ability of being able to read any room they are a part of.

Super-Situational can struggle with energy levels due to constant shifting and changing from situation to situation. Although this can be an effective leadership style it's also draining. Team members might also be a bit confused as they all get glimpses of different sides of the same vulnerable leader.

Abilities

- Adapts to any environment or situation
- Strong sense of self-awareness
- Can maintain diverse relationships
- Great at achieving goals and driving results

Weaknesses

- Can drain energy faster as a result of constant shifting, surveying, and scanning
- Might create confusion as different people see different sides
- Can be viewed as not authentic

Paul Markovich is the CEO of Blue Shield California. We met him previously in Chapter 6.

> I'm a situational vulnerable leader. Great leaders do what is needed for their people and the organization, and what is needed is dynamic; it changes and shifts. There may be times when you're in an existential crisis as a company and you're looking at a potential turnaround. The way you need to lead and how you're going to be a vulnerable leader in that circumstance can be very different than when you've got a very healthy company you're leading. When George Floyd happened, if I showed up to work talking about financial performance instead of saying "Oh, my God, I just witnessed a man being callously murdered in the street, and it has deeply affected me and made me also think very deeply about racism in this country, and what we can do to address it," then my team would look at me and wonder what's going on with me. Similarly, if I show up to work one day talking about diversity and inclusion or how I'm feeling while my business is a quarter away from insolvency, my team would look at me in that same way. It's not that these aren't important issues but people will be out of jobs if I can't turn things around. Leaders need to demonstrate competence here and have a plan. In terms of being an effective leader, it means knowing when and how to be vulnerable. It can help you be a more effective leader.

Balanced Beast

Balanced Beast has a balanced level of personal and professional vulnerability with everyone. They tend to not be as vulnerable as Captain Heart but instead are somewhere in between Work Warrior and Professor Personal. Unlike Super-Situational, who adjusts depending on the circumstance or the person, Balanced Beast is consistent across the board. I'm definitely more comfortable being a Balanced Beast in a work environment. My vulnerability is consistent in terms of things I share and am comfortable talking about, and it's the same with everyone I work with. This type of vulnerable leader will be just as open about a similar topic with a peer as they would be with a junior employee at the company.

Those who work with Balanced Beast feel like they have a good sense of who that leader is personally and professionally. This type of leader is viewed as being even-keeled and thrives in chaotic environments or during times of crisis. They are amazing emotional regulators, and people who work for Balanced Beast can feel more stable and secure.

The challenges with Balanced Beast vary depending on what the balance looks like. If this type of leader is comfortable with a balance that is more open and transparent about personal and professional vulnerability, then they will face the same headwinds as Captain Heart; however, if Balanced Beast is more comfortable with a conservative balance in which they don't share as much personally or professionally, then they will struggle with the same things as Wonder Worker.

Abilities

- Good at emotional regulation
- Clear thinking
- Great at conserving energy

Weaknesses

- Might not create strong relationships in certain situations, for example, if a peer feels that as a result of their relationship you should be more vulnerable with them than with others
- Can sometimes seem less authentic or even more robotic

At different times during our lives we may take on the role of a different superhero. In a way, all of these superheroes can live inside of us in some way. Being able to identify what kind of vulnerable leader you are and what kind of vulnerable leader you work with can help you determine where your strengths and weaknesses might be and how you may be able to address them.

The CEO of a large construction company told me the following: "I am consistent with everyone regardless of who they are or what their seniority level is. I can talk about some of my personal challenges or things I need help with at work with a new employee or one of our top executives. I take my job very seriously but not myself as a person. That to me is a part of leading with vulnerability, and having this consistent balance is a crucial part of my leadership style."

Although there are different types of vulnerable leaders, it doesn't mean that there are hard rules for them. I have found that most people think in terms of vulnerable leaders as either you are or you aren't, but this is not a practical or realistic approach to take.

People are most comfortable with Super-Situational (73%), followed by Wonder Worker (38%), Balanced Beast (27%), Professor Personal (20%), and Captain Heart (13%) (survey takers were able to select more than one response).

You may identify as more than one type of vulnerable leader, and you may also move from one to the other or even several times during your career. The best way to look at this is to ask yourself, "What type of vulnerable leader do I most identify with and why?" and "What kind of leader do you work with?" It's important to remember that all five of these superheroes are vulnerable leaders with their own abilities, strengths, and weaknesses, but they are all positive and impactful.

22

The Eight Attributes of Vulnerable Leaders

What makes up a vulnerable leader? At the beginning of the book I introduced eight attributes, five which comprise vulnerability and three which comprise leadership (see Figure 22.1):

- Self-awareness: understanding your thoughts, behaviors, actions, and emotions and how they affect you and those around you
- Self-compassion: being kind to yourself
- Empathy: seeing things from other people's perspectives
- Authenticity: being a single genuine version of yourself
- Integrity: being a moral and honest person with a clear set of personal values that guide how you behave
- Competence: being good at your job
- Self-confidence: belief in yourself and that you have the ability to grow and succeed
- Motivation: the drive to take action and improve

Figure 22.1   Eight attributes of vulnerable leaders

All of these attributes are important and powerful on their own, but when you bring them together and become a vulnerable leader, their impact is considerably greater than the sum of the parts. Many of these attributes overlap in terms of what they enable you to do, and oftentimes one will enable you to better harness another.

Here's how Bill Rogers, the chairman and CEO of Truist, a 55,000-person financial institution, frames this: "Self-confidence is gained through self-awareness, preparation, and reflection. Self-awareness provides the confidence that comes with knowing your purpose, values, and beliefs. Preparation creates a secondary layer of confidence on that foundation. And reflecting on past successes helps me gain insight."

Vulnerable leaders with the greatest impact are constantly working on developing all eight of these attributes.

Highly Competent

What's the biggest mistake you've ever made at work? I asked all of the CEOs I interviewed this question and one of the biggest and most costliest mistakes was made by Jacques van den Broek, the recently retired CEO of Randstad, a Dutch multinational human resources consulting firm with more than 42,000 employees. He made a $150 million mistake and, no, that's not why he retired. Jacques actually worked at the company for more than 34 years and more than 8 of those years were as CEO.

In the mid-1990s he made a big bet on HR outsourcing as the next big thing and he wanted his company to offer services in this space. They acquired companies, did a road show, and in total spent more than $150 million on something that ended up being a total failure because companies weren't ready to outsource their HR function. Jacques wasn't fired; in fact, he continued to lead Randstad for many years to come. It was a costly mistake but in the context of the company, which today has a market cap of about $10 billion. Jacques was very vulnerable when that mistake was made. He owned it, talked about it, and shared what he learned and what he planned to do going forward.

Since that mistake, Jacques has been instrumental in transforming and growing the company into the powerhouse that it is today with more than 5,000 branches and placing more than 2 million people in jobs every year. Jacques was clearly good at his job and he was also vulnerable. But what if Jacques were vulnerable and not good at his job? What if he made this same mistake, and under his tenure the company was going downhill as a result of his leadership and the decisions he made?

Piyush Gupta is the CEO of DBS Bank, which employs more than 35,000 employees. Since becoming CEO DBS has transformed from a leading Asian bank to being recognized as one of the best in the world. When I interviewed Gupta he addressed the role that competence and vulnerability play, highlighting that great leaders not only have to be competent in their jobs but also must have the ability to connect people. "Being able to show competence, capability, or success gives leaders the ability to be vulnerable without eroding morale or confidence in leadership ability. There's a lot of positive chemistry and magic that comes from being able to exhibit vulnerability. It creates trust and brings people closer together. This is important because, in my view, the ultimate lodestone of success as a leader is to be able to create a team that is greater than the sum of its parts. Vulnerability plus competence is a powerful combination for great leadership."

Leaders who are viewed as highly competent are able to go above and beyond what is expected of them. Highly competent leaders are always focused on growth in terms of training and development, and they focus on guiding others and helping them achieve success. Remember from Chapter 3 that in most instances leaders are already perceived as competent; that's why they are leaders. By leading with vulnerability their overall leadership effectiveness can increase dramatically, making them even more competent.

Is there a difference in perception between being vulnerable and being good at your job versus being vulnerable and not being good at your job? It turns out, there is.

In social psychology there is a concept called the pratfall effect, which was put forth in 1966 by Dr. Elliot Aronson, who is professor emeritus of my alma mater, the University of California, Santa Cruz. According to the pratfall effect, when people whom we perceive to be highly competent make a mistake, they appear more likable and approachable. However, when people whom we perceive to be incompetent make a mistake they appear less likable and approachable. As Elliot told me, "If you're already seen as mediocre, then taking a pratfall only adds to the impression of your mediocrity so then it becomes a liability rather than an asset. Similarly, it takes a terrific person and gives them an added boost, making them appear vulnerable and thus more likable, approachable, and even more competent and terrific."

As Nicolas Jimenez, CEO of BC Ferries, told me: "I want people to know when I make a mistake. It's a powerful way to create long-lasting and trusting bonds. Of course, there needs to be balance. You never just want to dwell on things you do poorly, but at the same time you also don't want to pretend that you are perfect. Admitting to mistakes is an incredibly powerful thing, and if you are competent, it makes you look much stronger and capable."

There is a small catch though: the context of the mistake matters. Let's say you are a financial advisor with a great track record and portfolio and you lose all of your client's money. If you're vulnerable with future prospective clients, it's doubtful they are going to want to work with you. It will take time for you to build your competence and trust levels back up to a point where you can be more vulnerable with them (see Figure 22.2).

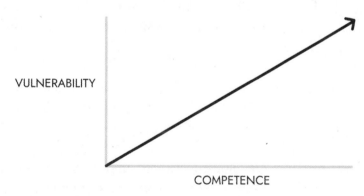

Figure 22.2 Vulnerability and competence

According to Dr. Aronson, "Vulnerability is a double-edged sword; it can be very positive if you are in the company of people who are inclined to like and respect you. But if you're swimming with sharks, vulnerability can be a disaster because they smell blood. You don't always want to be vulnerable in the presence of someone who is out to get you."

Again, context matters and there is no rule in terms of how big or small the mistake has to be, but it's safe to say it almost always can't be something that causes irreparable harm or damage. Spilling coffee on yourself or making a mistake in a presentation is not the same thing as bankrupting a business.

Competence is a unique attribute in that it is the most important one out of the eight to obtain. Competence has a very direct relationship with vulnerability. The more competent you are, the more vulnerable you can be and the more vulnerable you are the more competent you become. Even if you have all of the other attributes, if you do not have a high level of competence, then you will not be able to achieve positive outcomes by being vulnerable. There is no substitute for someone being good at their job.

Jeff Immelt is the former CEO of GE, and one of the things he teaches aspiring leaders is the importance of embracing seemingly countervailing ideas at the same time: "Leadership can be filled with paradoxes. Vulnerability and competence are not separate things; they are interconnected and you cannot have one without the other. You have to be vulnerable and you have to be good at your job. The more competent you are, the more vulnerable you should be to connect with your people and level the playing field and the more vulnerable you are, the more you should grow in your competence as you learn new things and grow as a leader."

It's important to distinguish between seniority and competence. There are plenty of senior leaders who are not competent, and there are plenty of entry- and mid-level employees who are very competent. Being highly competent simply means being good at your job as determined by the objective criteria inside of your organization and the subjective judgment of your peers. For example, if you are in sales, being a highly competent salesperson might mean that you are closing a certain number of deals and bringing in a certain amount of revenue. It also means that your peers view you in a generally positive light. You close deals in ethical ways, you treat your peers and customers well, and you have a good reputation. You don't have to be the senior VP of sales to prove that you are competent, although the idea is that your competence will help you get that role. In fact, there are many highly competent professionals who often decline promotions because they don't want to be responsible for leading others, yet they are still very good at their jobs. Competence is not the same thing as seniority.

Steve Bilt, the CEO of Smile Brands, a dental services provider with more than 7,500 employees, gave me a helpful analogy for competence:

> If you're in sixth grade asking about fourth grade math, then you need to be aware you're asking about fourth grade math. You have to know what your peer skills and mindsets should be for your position. Own and accept that if you are behind you, you must be accountable for catching yourself up. Ask for a tutor, use your own time, and make the investment. But if you don't take accountability and you just keep showing up each day asking the same remedial questions, then you are going to end up in a situation where people will question whether you should be in your position.

Does this mean that if you aren't good at your job you can't be vulnerable? Definitely not. We don't all start off automatically being good at our jobs; it takes time, training, and learning before we reach a desired level of competence. The important thing is that you actually do learn, grow, and develop. Remember, being a vulnerable leader is about vulnerability plus leadership—don't forget that second piece of the equation. This means that if you aren't growing, learning, or getting better, then there is an issue that needs to be addressed.

But let's not take this out of context or be insensitive to our team members, a mistake that I recently made. We all go through difficult and tragic times in our lives that affect our performance and leadership at work.

For example, if someone is going through a divorce and they share this vulnerability as a reason to explain why they are struggling, don't respond with, "Hey, there are plenty of fish in the sea. It's time to move on and get back on track." More than ever we need compassion, empathy, and kindness at work.

Allen is a designer I've worked with for more than a decade. He designed several of my book covers (including this one), images I use on social media, my websites, and all sorts of other content (including the stuff for this book), and we've never met in person. He's based in the Philippines and does awesome work.

Toward the end of my writing this book I was under quite a bit of stress as I was trying to meet my deadline while juggling a lot of other projects that were coming my way. Although I'm usually very cool-headed and understanding, I became a bit frustrated with Allen because he wasn't turning things around as quickly and with the same level of quality that he usually does. This in turn made me more anxious and stressed. Instead of checking in with him to see how he was doing I sent him the following Skype message when he was offline:

"Hey, Allen, I hope you and your family are doing okay. I haven't heard back from you on the design stuff, a few things are all past due, and I feel like I have to be your assistant and keep checking in with you. Please let me know if you're not able to get the designs/images done and I can find someone else to help, but I can't keep checking in with you every few days on stuff. It takes up a lot of my time and energy."

Sure, that first sentence sounded nice, but it was there to not make me sound like a complete jerk. In fact, when I was first going to write this to Allen, I didn't even have that sentence in there. But a jerk is actually how I felt when Allen responded to me.

Hey Jacob, thanks! We are safe now and I think the typhoon is almost out of the country. I understand your situation and I deeply apologize for the delay these past couple of weeks. As much as possible, I try to avoid excuses and having my work be affected by my personal life but the last two weeks have been very stressful and unfortunate for my family. Olivia got sick last week and now Ira is dealing with heavy coughing this week. It's tough but thankfully, Olivia is almost 100% while Ira is taking antibiotics already. I'll be more transparent with situations like this and avoid affecting your time and effort negatively with delays. I'll be able to focus more. I'm really passionate in helping you with this book as I saw how much you want this to be your goal for next year. I want to help make that a success and I'll make sure these lapses will not happen again. In any case I failed, I will understand if you find someone else for help. Sorry for the trouble!"

I felt like someone punched me in the stomach. Here I was assuming that he was slacking off, meanwhile his city was getting pummeled by a typhoon and he had flooding issues, his newborn daughter was sick, and his wife was dealing with a heavy cough. No wonder his work was struggling, because he was struggling, and I never made the effort to ask or find out. Knowing what someone on your team is going through is important in order for leaders to tell if there is really an issue with competence or if it's something else. This is why it's crucial for leaders to know their people as human beings and not just as workers.

Larry Gies, whom we met in Chapter 2, shared the following with me:

Our employee surveys show that the number-one thing that our teams want from their leader is that their leader cares about them as people. There is someone hurting in your orbit each and every day. If you don't show them it's okay to reach out and ask for help, you are missing a huge opportunity to have an impact and show them you care. Your teammates will not reach out and ask for help if you don't show them first that it's okay to do this. You are their leader and they are watching your every move to determine the ground rules of your organization and how you interact on a day-to-day basis. Before every meeting and at the end of every meeting across our companies, we share a "mission/culture moment"—that is, one of the meeting participants volunteers to tell a story of a mission/culture moment at Madison, [and] a leader connected with the team and/or put mission before profits.

Don't use vulnerability as a crutch for competence. If you are not capable, able, or qualified to do the work you are doing and you aren't making the necessary effort required to get better, then you can't keep saying, "I'm sorry I made a mistake" or "I need help doing this." At some point you are either able to do the job or you aren't.

Simply put, there is no substitute for being good at your job. Competence is usually the easiest attribute to develop and most of us know how to develop it. It's no secret that competence comes from hard work, training, dedication, and putting in the time to master your craft.

Steve Hilton is the executive chairman of Meritage Homes. Here is what he told me about competence and vulnerability: "I don't know many people who are good at their jobs who are not vulnerable leaders. Being a vulnerable leader means you want to learn, grow, and connect with your people. How can you be good at your job and lead through change if you don't do these things?"

How to get competence:

- Practice your craft.
- Participate in ongoing development and training programs.
- Ask for feedback and implement what you learn.
- Join peer groups and associations.
- Focus on mastery, meaning improvement.
- Work hard.

Self-Awareness

A very successful businessman visits a Zen master to get some help. Although he was very successful, he didn't find much connection and meaning in his life. The businessman sits down with the Zen master and starts unloading all of his problems and issues. The Zen master tries to provide some wisdom and guidance but the businessman keeps interrupting him and interjecting his own thoughts and opinions. After a few minutes the Zen master gets up to get some tea for himself and his guest. He poured the tea for the businessman but after the cup filled, he kept pouring, causing the cup to overflow. "Stop, the cup is full!" the businessman shouts. The Zen master stopped pouring and said, "Similarly, you are too full of your own opinions. You want my help, but you have no room in your own cup to receive my words."

We are often so stuck in our own heads that we don't even open ourselves up to the feedback or the wisdom of those around us. If we are so full of our own thoughts and judgments, then we will never see the Zen master and their wisdom, and anyone around you can be the Zen master with something to teach you.

Self-awareness is about understanding yourself, including your passions, fears, strengths, and weaknesses. It's also about understanding how your actions, thoughts, motivations, and feelings affect those around you. It's just as much internal as it is external.[1]

Nancy McKinstry, whom we met in Chapter 11, is a big proponent of self-awareness. "You can't be authentic if you are not self-aware. How can you be transparent and open, talk about your goals, or share how you are influencing change without self-awareness? You cannot change or be vulnerable if you don't know yourself and how you impact others."

Leading with vulnerability requires a combination of self-reflection but also asking for and listening to the feedback you get from others about you. Benjamin Franklin used to keep a balance sheet of his personal traits, strengths, and weaknesses. Anything positive was considered an asset and anything negative was considered a liability. Whenever he learned something new or developed in a positive way, he would write those things down in his assets column so that he could better understand his personal net worth. Ideally, he wanted to see his assets column grow and his liabilities column shrink. This is an exercise he would do on a regular basis, and it forced him to reflect on who he was and how well he knew himself.

Scott Farquhar is the cofounder and co-CEO of Atlassian, an Australian software company with more than 10,000 employees:

> About a year ago I got a 360 review from my team. There was a lot of really tough feedback in there about how I show up to work and the behaviors I exhibited, which were causing harm to other people. These were things I was doing unintentionally. This was a very vulnerable moment for me. I actually keep that 360 feedback with me at all times. I was told that people didn't think I valued them. There would be times where I would disagree with a team member in front of others and continue to press the issue. It feels pretty terrible when your leader doesn't defend you in front of others and, even worse, comes after you. Nobody wants to feel abandoned and I realized that's exactly what I was doing to my team. I was abandoning them instead of standing up for them.
>
> This made me really self-reflect on who I am as a leader and how I show up and also how others see me. This is something I and all leaders need to be more aware of. Paying attention to not just how you view yourself but how you actually show up and how others see you.

One way you can think of self-awareness is internal vulnerability, in other words, being aware of and okay with who you are and how you are. Being able to be vulnerable with yourself is just as important as being vulnerable with others.

How to obtain self-awareness:

- Reflect on your own strengths, weaknesses, passions, fears, hopes, and emotions. Put together your own balance sheet.
- Get candid feedback from those around you on how you are perceived and how you show up.
- Meditate or journal to get a better sense of your thoughts and feelings.
- Try taking personality tests so you can get to know yourself better.
- Surround yourself with a few people you trust who will be honest with you when you need to hear feedback that could be painful.[2]

Self-Confidence

Being confident in yourself is not the same thing as being arrogant. Being arrogant means you have an exaggerated version of your importance, your abilities, or your impact. It's often what happens as a result of a distorted version of self-awareness. This is why it's important not only to know yourself but also to understand how other people see you. Confidence, however, is about believing in yourself. It's trusting in yourself and your abilities and having an overall positive view of yourself. It also means that you are open to feedback from others and can admit when you have made a mistake.

Unfortunately, what happens to many leaders around the world is that confidence turns into arrogance because another ingredient is added: an uncontrolled ego:

$$Ego + Confidence = Arrogance$$

Using a basketball analogy, being arrogant means you always want the ball because you think you're the only one who can score. Being confident means you pass the ball because you know others can score but that you want the ball when the game is tied with three seconds on the clock because you are confident in your ability to make the game-winning shot.

The good news is that self-awareness will also help you become more self-confident. Sabir Sami is the CEO of fast-food chain KFC Global, which has more than 820,000 team members. He understands the connection between self-confidence and vulnerability: "It seems like a contradiction but one does need to have self-confidence to be vulnerable. At times of fear I ask myself, 'What's the worst that can happen?' The answer is usually far below my imagined fears. I really wish I had more role models early in my career who demonstrated that vulnerability; it would have helped me so much in my journey. I hope more leaders lead this way to make the journey easier and better for younger professionals."

Being self-confident doesn't mean that you know all the answers, that you have the best ideas, or that you will never make mistakes or get knocked down. Self-confidence is what enables you to get back up after you've been knocked down. It enables you to take chances, speak up, and take on the tough challenges and opportunities that other people might run away from. Self-confidence means you have your own back and you accept yourself for who you are.

How to get self-confidence:

- Surround yourself with people who lift you up.
- Focus on your strengths.
- Invest in preparation whether it be for a meeting, presentation, project, and so on. Prepare before you play.
- Practice.

Self-Compassion

When my wife and I get in an argument and I say something mean, she will respond with, "I know you're saying that because you aren't treating yourself very kindly right now," and she's right. What Blake is really saying is that when I'm being mean and judgmental of her, I'm actually talking to and about myself. I'm not able to be vulnerable and connect with her because I'm not being self-compassionate. I always brushed these comments off but it turns out she's right.

Dr. Anna Bruk is the chair of micro-sociology and social psychology at the University of Mannheim and she has done some pioneering work in vulnerability. According to Dr. Bruk being vulnerable actually starts with being self-compassionate, that is, treating yourself with the same kindness that you would treat a good friend. It also comes with accepting and understanding that perfection doesn't exist and being imperfect is a part of what makes us human.

But wait a minute. Why does treating yourself kindly affect your ability to ask for help, to admit you made a mistake, or to share something personal about yourself? Because, as Dr. Bruk explained to me, it gives you a safe place to land. What happens if you are vulnerable with someone and they don't respond in the way you think or hope? You're probably going to be embarrassed, flustered, or upset, right? Self-compassion is the safety net that says you know everything will be okay because, remember, it's talking to yourself in a kind way. If something doesn't go as planned, instead of saying, "Wow, I can't believe you just shared that with your team; they're going to think you're an idiot," you say, "It's okay that things didn't go as planned; you took a chance and learned something in the process, and tomorrow is another day." That ability to be kind to yourself gives you safety and allows you to be vulnerable. Remember the learning moments that I talked about previously? Self-compassion is a critical component to help you reach them.

On the flipside, without the safety net of self-compassion, it can be very hard to express vulnerability. Instead of revealing that we are scared, we can become unreasonably demanding of others. Instead of directly asking for help, we may get mad that others didn't guess our needs. After all, how we treat others is oftentimes a reflection of how we treat ourselves. If you are working with a leader who is rude, closed off, puts you down, and isn't vulnerable, then chances are quite high that this leader treats herself unkindly and is avoiding the discomfort of showing vulnerability. However, as Dr. Bruk cautioned when we spoke, this isn't meant to be an excuse for treating other people poorly. Meaning, you can't just say, "I'm mean to myself. That's why I'm so mean to everyone else." That's not a justification and it's not okay. Rather it's a reason to learn to treat oneself well so that one can treat others well, too.

Bill Rogers, the chairman and CEO of Truist Financial Corporation with 55,000 employees, told me, "I regularly carve out some quiet, meditative time for myself. And I remind myself that I am human, give myself clemency for imperfection, and strive to learn from my mistakes."

Self-compassion can take many forms, including positive self-talk, meditation, giving yourself time and space each day to reflect, doing daily gratitudes, journaling, telling yourself that you will be okay, or even going on walks in nature.

Jim Fitterling is the chairman and CEO of Dow Chemical Company, which has more than 35,000 employees around the world. He shared a lovely story with me about self-compassion:

> Self-compassion is often the hardest type of compassion to achieve, in my experience. I believe we often hold ourselves up to a different and higher standard than we set for others and—if we don't reach those high standards—we are too hard on ourselves. I have a colleague who said he has a son who is super-kind to others, very compassionate and thoughtful. But tough on himself.
>
> And my colleague said he told his son: "My greatest wish for you is that you are as kind to yourself as you are to others." I thought that was a great approach—we need to show ourselves the same kind of grace and empathy that we demonstrate with others and allow ourselves to fail every now and then, knowing that we're all human and that failure is often just one more step toward success.

Jim's story reminds me of how I try to be with my kids. I make a lot of mistakes as a dad, husband, son, friend, and as a business owner, and I know that my kids are always watching to see how I will react. I used to really struggle with positive self-talk and self-compassion but I'm now much better at it because I know that what my kids see they will do, and I want them to be kind to themselves.

How to get self-compassion:

- Practice positive self-talk.
- Invest in physical, emotional, mental, and spiritual self-care.
- Create a regular self-compassion routine.
- Don't ignore the critical voice inside of your head. Acknowledge that it is there and tell that voice that you are choosing a different route.

Empathy

Mark S. Hoplamazian, the president and CEO of Hyatt Hotels Corporation whom we met in Chapter 3, always thought he was an empathetic person. Then he did various psychographic tests and found out that his inherent inclination to practice empathy was actually quite low, below 50 on a scale going up to 100. He was shocked and he rejected the results.

He went home and decided to talk to his kids about it and they gave him some pretty candid feedback, which was both devastating and impactful to Mark. They told him that even though he thinks he is empathetic and present with them, they find that when they drive to school together in the mornings, he isn't. He's often on his phone at red lights and his kids have to tell him when the light turns green. Mark wasn't empathetic to how this made his kids feel and he didn't put himself in their shoes:

This conversation with my kids about my level of empathy was so impactful. I was pretty devastated. When I dropped them off at school the following day, I told them that I had been thinking about what they told me and that I was going to really work on it. I realized that you can really be at risk if you're not seeing yourself clearly. In my life, my children have the best capability of bringing my feet and planting them firmly on the ground, or sometimes slamming them on the ground. That really did have a huge impact on me and really vaulted me into a very different pathway for how I lead and practice empathy.

The impact of vulnerability on empathy is massive. When leaders often or always show a willingness to be vulnerable, they are 17.7× more likely to listen and respond with empathy than those who rarely or never display vulnerability.

Prior to the pandemic, I was asked to speak to the leadership teams of two different financial institutions in New York City. Both fierce competitors. Before going on stage, I usually take a few minutes to call or text my wife to check in on her back home. She usually tells me to smile and enjoy myself before my talk. When she speaks at conferences, the roles are reversed, and I'm the one telling her to smile and have fun.

At the first of the two companies, I'm texting my wife when I see a new employee approach one of the top executives at the company who was sitting on a couch a few feet away from me checking his email. The employee goes over to the executive and says, "Hey, you're James Smith, right?" The executive looks up and says, "I am. What's up?" The employee then begins to share that she has been struggling with her leader, she feels overwhelmed, and that she's not sure she belongs at the company. Without even looking up from his computer this executive says, "Don't worry about it. You're just having new employee jitters. You'll be fine; good luck!"

A few days later I'm speaking for their largest competitor.

As usual, I'm texting with my wife and I see one of the top executives sitting a few feet away from me drinking coffee and doing something on his phone. One of her employees comes up to her and says, "You're Joanne Williams, right?" She looks up and says, "I am. What's up?" The employee then proceeds to tell her that he has really been struggling in his role, that he feels overwhelmed with work, and that he doesn't feel like he belongs there. The executive takes a sip of her coffee, puts away her phone and invites this new employee to sit down. She then proceeds to tell him about when she first started working at the company, how she felt the exact same way, and what she did to overcome that feeling. She ended the conversation with "My door is always open to you, and here is how you can reach me if you ever need me." I've never seen such a quick transformation in a human being before. This new employee walked away with a big smile, a pep in his step, and a completely different attitude that was clearly visible.

The first example is what sympathy looks like, when someone tells you "I'm sorry; you'll be fine." The second example is what empathy looks like. Are you able to understand the feelings and emotions of those around you and do you have the ability to actually put yourself in their shoes to see their point of view? Imagine if you could pause time, take yourself out of your body, and put it into someone else's body to feel and experience things the way they are. This is what empathy is all about—creating that connection with someone else in a way that ultimately creates a powerful level of trust.

To practice empathy, you don't need to experience the same thing as someone else; you just need to experience the emotion. Maybe you never experienced getting fired from a job but your friend did. You can still relate to the feeling of disappointment, anger, and perhaps even embarrassment because those are emotions you have no doubt felt before.

Ravi Saligram is the CEO of Newell Brands, the 29,000-person company behind household names like Sharpie, Rubbermaid, and Coleman.

"In the past, leaders placed a very high value on IQ and, yes, it's still important. But in today's world I believe that EQ [emotional intelligence] is even more valuable. Specifically empathy, which is very much related to vulnerability. The ability to put yourself in someone else's shoes in a genuine way is so valuable and impactful, yet it's not something we are trained to do. This is a muscle inside of companies, and the more leaders can build and train this muscle the better we will all be. Inside of my company I have seen how important empathy is for teamwork, collaboration, and trust. Being a vulnerable leader is a strength, and empathy helps you get there".

How to get empathy:

- Focus on the things you have in common with other people but respect the differences.
- Recognize the emotions in others, recall a time when you felt that same emotion, and name it.
- Surround yourself with people who are not like you.
- Remove judgment.

Authenticity

The most common response I got back when I asked the more than 100 CEOs to define what it means to be a vulnerable leader was "authenticity." When probed further, this was defined as being a single version of you. Although this is an important component for unlocking the vulnerability superpower, it's entirely different than vulnerability. Remember that previously in Chapter 2 I defined being a vulnerable leader as a leader who intentionally opens himself up to the potential of emotional harm while taking action (when possible) to create a positive outcome. You don't need to be authentic to do that. Jack Welch was authentic and so was Steve Ballmer. They arguably wore their emotions on their sleeves but were they known for intentionally opening themselves up to the potential of emotional harm? Absolutely not. Being authentic and being vulnerable are certainly intertwined but they are not the same thing.

One of the most powerful stories on authenticity came to me from Jim Fitterling, the CEO of Dow Chemical Company, whom we met earlier.

> The most vulnerable I ever felt was when I came out. I had previously been diagnosed with Stage IV cancer and began seeing my life through an entirely different lens. It was during that process—of struggling through recovery—that I knew if I was going to grow further—as a human and as a leader—I was going to have to bring more of my authentic self to the equation. That part of me I had kept walled off. That's when I decided to come out as a gay individual. It was, easily, the most vulnerable time of my life because I didn't know how my colleagues would react.
>
> I began slowly. I talked with each member of our board of directors one-on-one. Then our leadership team. And then our entire company. It wasn't easy. But the process of being vulnerable lifted a huge burden from me and allowed me to refocus my energies away from being who I wasn't to simply being me. And in turn, helping others be themselves. My experience through that entire process confirmed for me what I've heard many others say: that the fear of being vulnerable is just that—fear. And mostly misplaced fear. I was extremely heartened by the positive and supportive reaction I received from my colleagues. My internal fears were replaced by genuine appreciation for me as a person.
>
> Allowing myself to be vulnerable opened up a fantastic new avenue of growth for me. At the same time, I felt we needed to create more of a culture of vulnerability at Dow. I knew how powerful it was for me and saw this as a critical part of our company's growth and culture going forward. That culture can't just be lip service. At Dow our culture starts with

our core values of integrity, respect for people, and protecting our planet. Vulnerability comes with each. And your people need to see you living it from the top of the organization and to feel encouraged and supported to also bring their authentic self to work. And to do that you have to be willing to be out in front of it. When you are, great things can happen with the culture of your teams.

Being authentic means being sincere and genuine in the things you say and do. If you tell someone they did a good job, you mean it and aren't saying it to be sarcastic.

How to get authenticity:

- Define your personal set of values and stick to them.
- Speak up.
- Share how you're feeling.
- Be honest with yourself and those around you.

Motivation

You don't need motivation to be vulnerable, but you need motivation to lead with vulnerability. Tomorrow, you can show up to work and spill your heart to everyone and anyone who is willing to listen, and then what? Going back to our Vulnerable Leader Equation, this is simply being vulnerable. I certainly don't recommend you do this, but you can.

To get to that positive outcome, you need motivation, which is your internal driving force for getting to that positive outcome. For example, you're in the middle of a meeting with your peers and your leader turns to you and says, "How do you think we should go about solving this tricky problem that we're faced with?" You think for a moment and instead of saying, "I don't know" (vulnerable) you say, "I'm not really sure what to do; let me think about this a little bit and I'll get back to you with some ideas (leading with vulnerability)."

But now you need action. Motivation is what actually gets you to explore those new ideas. You can't learn, grow, and develop if you don't actually take some sort of action to do those things.

Gary Smith is the CEO of Ciena, an 8,000-person networking systems, software, and services company: "You must have the desire to learn and engage and to help yourself and those around you. Vulnerability means accepting that you need help or support but you as an individual need to be motivated to take action, solve a problem, or create an outcome based on the help or support you receive; otherwise, what's the point? Motivation is a crucial aspect of being a vulnerable leader as opposed to just being vulnerable."

How to get motivation:

- Create personal and professional goals that you revisit on a regular basis.
- Surround yourself with people who are also motivated.
- Start small and make pursuing your goals a part of a regular routine.

Integrity

This really comes down to being a moral and honest person with a clear set of personal values that guide how you behave. Integrity is what gets your friends and peers to say things like "so-and-so is really a good person."

Employees look to guidance from leaders on how to behave, and they will emulate the behaviors that leaders exhibit. If a leader doesn't have integrity, meaning they do things such as cut corners, stab people in the back, lie about their wins and failures, and don't treat people with respect, then employees will think it's okay for them to do the same. This creates a toxic environment for everyone.

In a recent episode of my podcast, "Great Leadership with Jacob Morgan," I interviewed Jeff Raider, who is the cofounder of Warby Parker and the co-CEO and cofounder of Harry's, a 1,000-person consumer packaged goods company that creates beauty and grooming products for men and women (through their Flamingo brand). Jeff told me a story of how they were coming out with a new razor with a dark-colored metal and that they could also make that same razor in chrome. One of their partners said that they could easily charge more for that chrome razor and everyone on the team was excited about the idea of making more money. Jeff asked to see the two razors side-by-side. He felt that they looked almost identical. He then challenged his team by asking why a customer would want to pay $5 extra for that chrome razor and if that was the right thing to do. Jeff told the team they weren't going to be doing that. It all came down to integrity, which is what creates trust among his employees and customers.

Nancy McKinstry from Wolters Kluwer (Chapter 3) and Penny Pennington from Edward Jones (Chapters 2 and 7) are two CEOs for whom integrity is a critical element of their leadership styles. Here's Nancy: "I have a very strong line on integrity, which to me means knowing what I care about and value and where my lines are and which lines I'm not willing to cross. I treat people with respect and if you name a job, I probably did it at some point in my life because I didn't have a lot of money and I put myself through school. I know what it's like to struggle, to work hard, and to respect others, and that is how I treat others. Integrity is having a strong moral character, which is very important to me."

For Penny, integrity is the driving force that helps her make decisions. Here's what she told me:

A lot of leaders think that integrity is just about telling the truth, and that's certainly a part of it but it's not the full picture. Integrity is about the problems and challenges that you decide to take on and the actions that you as a leader take whether they are big or small. That is how your integrity manifests itself and how it is visible to the world. Integrity is where I am using my purpose to the fullest, to do everything I can to make the world a better place and to not leave anything on the table to make that happen. Integrity and purpose go hand in hand, and you cannot be a vulnerable leader without having integrity.

Leaders with integrity are trustworthy, ethical, and honest. How to get integrity:

- Do what you say you're going to do.
- Define and communicate your values with others.
- Do the right thing even though it's not always the most profitable thing.
- Surround yourself with other people who have high integrity.

Do you need to possess these attributes in order to be vulnerable? No. Nothing is stopping you from being vulnerable when you show up to work tomorrow. But, if you want to be a vulnerable leader, then these eight attributes will greatly enhance the likelihood that your vulnerability will yield a positive outcome.

23

The Vulnerability Wheel

Leading with vulnerability is the most powerful thing that you as a leader can do. Developing the eight attributes helps you unlock that power, but the vulnerability wheel helps you harness that power so it has the highest chance of being received the right way and creating a positive impact.

There is a right and wrong way to be vulnerable at work and the right way does require some structure for it. Context matters.

Recall the Vulnerable Leader Equation:

Vulnerable + Leader = Leading with Vulnerability

The leadership component means that you need to pay special attention to several elements that make up the Vulnerable Leader Wheel, a framework that will walk you through five elements you should consider before deciding to be vulnerable (see Figure 23.1).

Figure 23.1   The Vulnerable Leader Wheel

You can't always control all of the elements in the wheel; for example, something might come out during a meeting with your peers or during a spontaneous moment of connection with a team member. There is absolutely nothing wrong with those and they can be beautiful and meaningful experiences.

My goal with this framework isn't to imply that every moment of vulnerability needs to be analyzed, dissected, scripted, and presented as if it's been run through a public relations team. This framework is designed as more of a mental checklist of things you should consider when you can. Several CEOs I interviewed told me that they apply this approach intuitively instead of consciously thinking through each element.

Intention

Vulnerable leaders don't show up to work each day treating their teams and their organization like a big therapy session. They are vulnerable with a purpose. For example, if a leader talks about a personal challenge or struggle, it's with the (authentic) purpose of creating connection and building relationships. If a leader asks for help or admits to a mistake, it's done with the purpose of learning and improving. Being vulnerable with intention is an important aspect of being a vulnerable leader. Intention sits at the very core of the wheel; without it, everything else falls apart and those around you will just be left with more questions than answers. Intention is about reaching a goal and should always be centered on progress or growth. You can easily tell if that's the case because you will notice that your intention will be described with positive adjectives, such as *build, create, learn, become, grow.*

Judy McReynolds is the CEO of ArcBest, an integrated logistics company with more than 14,000 employees. Here's what she told me about intention: "As a leader I need to have intention when being vulnerable. There needs to be some kind of purpose in mind such as getting to new ideas, learning something new, solving a problem, or connecting with someone on a human level. For me the intention is usually around learning since I consider myself a lifelong learner."

Ask yourself, "Why do you want to be vulnerable and what are you hoping to achieve?

Who Are You Being Vulnerable With?

Peter Strebel is the chairman and former president of Omni Hotels & Resorts, with more than 23,000 employees. He told me: "You have to be aware of who you are vulnerable with and listen for cues and pay attention to signs. Understanding who you can be vulnerable with is a little bit of a science but much more of an art."

Peter's point is an important one. Not everyone has your best interest at heart and not everyone is capable or willing to receive your vulnerability in a positive way. Knowing your audience is crucial.

Outside of writing leadership books like the one you are reading right now, I speak at dozens of conferences and events each year. I need to know my audiences. If I'm speaking in a foreign country, I'll speak slower and use localized examples instead of focusing on US companies. I also pay attention to cultural differences in terms of how people interact and say hello. If I'm speaking to a company that I know is looking to improve their approach to leadership, then I'm not going to spend a lot of time talking about technology. And if I'm speaking with a smaller, growing organization, then I won't assume they have an endless budget where they can invest in anything and everything.

Similarly, if you are being vulnerable with someone, it's important to know whom you are being vulnerable with. Is it with a new employee who might feel uncomfortable? A trusted peer who will give you candid feedback? Or a shark who is coming for you? It's never advisable to be vulnerable with everyone and paying attention to cues and signs is crucial. For example, is the other person following along intently or are their eyes glazed over? Is their body language open or do they look annoyed and uncomfortable? Are they acknowledging what you are saying with nods and follow-up questions or are they silent? Paying attention to the signs will help you decide if it's safe to keep going or if you need to stop and transition to something else.

Kate Robertson is the cofounder of One Young World, which focuses on creating great young leaders around the world. Prior to that she was the global president for Havas Worldwide, which today has about 20,000 employees.

One day in Paris, the company was having an executive committee dinner for 22 executives, all of whom reported to Kate. In the middle of the dinner, one of the top male executives gives Kate a gift in front of everyone, a book in a brown paper bag. It turned out to be a very inappropriate gift. Kate took out the book and was shocked . . . it was a coffeetable book of erect penises.

Kate told me she felt "vulnerable as hell in that moment" as she knew everyone was looking at her, but she didn't show it, instead she put the book back into the bag and slid it across the table back to the executive who gave it to her and said, "I don't want that; thanks very much" and carried on with the conversation she was having.

According to Kate, "When I look back at it now, I should have gone to town on it, and gotten that person fired, but I didn't because I could not show any kind of vulnerability. The fact is, I was put in that situation as a woman and I was supposed to laugh and giggle and think it's funny. But actually, I was being humiliated."

Kate recognized that this was not a person she could be vulnerable with. She didn't feel safe because this executive clearly didn't have her best interests in mind. He was trying to humiliate her and bring her down.

Even though she felt vulnerable on the inside she didn't let it show. By not reporting this person not only did it hurt Kate but also all of the other women who will work with this . . . idiot

The Circle of Trust

Here's an example of something you shouldn't do. You just got a leadership role working for an 8,000-person technology company. It's day one and you show up for a team meeting with some of your peers and direct reports. Your turn comes to share a bit about yourself and who you are and you say, "Hi, everyone, I'm really excited to be here. To be honest I don't know how I got this job. Even my wife thinks I'm in over my head! I was let go from my last company and I'm just looking forward to this fresh start and implementing some of my new ideas, which I hope will work out better than they did at my last job. When I'm not working I like to go out and party and I'm in therapy to figure out how to be a better dad. Anyway, that's just a little about me. Thanks for having me, and go team!!"

There are a lot of problems with this statement, which could potentially be career-ending. However, if you break some of the things down, there are lots of things there that could be said to members of a team whom you really trust. For example, that you are working on yourself and trying to be a better parent or that you may be experiencing imposter syndrome. A small group of people whom you trust and who are genuinely interested in your growth and success is important for leaders to have. These are people who can challenge you, give you candid feedback, act as a sounding board, and share insights and guidance to help you achieve your desired goals.

Lara Abrash, the Chair of Deloitte US, is another leader who has depended on her circle of trust for personal and professional success. Her circle of trust consists of a handful of partners at the firm and her husband. Some of the partners she has known for a few years and others she's known for more than 30 years. She believes in creating a circle of trust composed of people of varying seniority levels and age groups:

> Some have seen me evolve over the course of my career, but what's really critical is that they not only know me, but they also have a finger on the pulse of the business. It's also important that they are not "yes" people and that they have a different way of looking at things, sometimes even contrarian to how I see things. I'm also very clear and transparent with them—I have told them that I value their input and that I'm going to test things out on them from time to time. Sometimes I go to all of them, sometimes I may just go to two or three, depending on what the topic is. They know they're valued voices to me and that I want their thoughtful and honest feedback.

Ask yourself, "Do I know whom I am being vulnerable with and do I trust them? Do I have a circle of people whom I trust, have a good relationship with, and who are invested in my success that I can share things with in confidence?

When

Timing matters. If your leader is about to get in an elevator, you probably don't want to say, "By the way, I really messed something up with a client," as the doors are closing. There is a time and a place to share things, and as a vulnerable leader it's important for you to pay attention to them. If you're about to go into an important meeting with a prospect, it's probably not a good idea to say, "I've never worked on a project like this before, and I'm not sure if I can meet your goals." However, once the project is completed, ideally successfully, then it can be quite powerful to share, "When we first started working together I was really nervous that I wouldn't be able to meet your goals. I learned a lot from working together." In both situations the vulnerability is there but the timing of what you share can change the outcome, in this case, landing a project or not.

Jason McGowan from Crumbl Cookies, whom we met in Chapter 3, has a unique approach to this:

> One thing that's been really effective for me is scheduled vulnerability. In my experience if I'm vulnerable right after something happens, then sometimes my judgment and motives can be questioned. However, if I schedule time for one-on-one discussions when I have time to think through what I want to say and when I want to say it, then it's more intentional and purposeful and the other person also opens up. Of course, I'm vulnerable at other times as well, but actually having time for this is very powerful for me and my team. Timing makes all the difference to how you and your message come across and how it resonates with others.

Ask yourself, "Is now the best time for me to be vulnerable or should I plan for something in the future?"

Tone

It's not always what you say, it's how you say it. Tone makes a huge difference in how your message gets across, and it can make the difference between being perceived as vulnerable, aggressive, arrogant, or something else. When you say, "I need help," that can come across as you would imagine it would—that you are genuinely asking for help—or it can come across in a sarcastic way to imply "are you kidding me?" Similarly, "I don't know" can come across as either dismissive or disrespectful, or it can come across as genuine.

Jeff Guldner is the CEO and chairman at Pinnacle West Capital Corporation, a US utility holding company with more than 6,000 employees. He shared a technique that one of his senior leaders uses:

> There's a great senior leader at the company who starts his questions off with "I'm probably not understanding this correctly, but here's what I think you're saying." This has been an interesting technique that he has developed that really humanizes him. His tone is genuine and signals that he is really looking to learn and understand. He could just as easily say, "What you're saying doesn't make sense," which is a completely different tone and approach. One is vulnerable and the other is defensive and aggressive. When he's talking to frontline supervisors or managers you can watch this leader and actually see people around him becoming more at ease because of his tone.

In the eyes and ears of the people you work with, perception is reality. This is an especially powerful thing to remember. If you find that people don't want to do what you ask, they don't understand what you're saying, they aren't connecting with your message, or they frequently don't agree with you, then the culprit is oftentimes not what you are saying but how you are saying it. Tone can also be used to describe your body language and overall demeanor. We communicate with all parts of our body, not just our mouths.

Whenever my wife and I get in an argument, her most common issue with me isn't what I say, it's how I say it because even though the words may seem neutral or kind, the tone signals aggressiveness, ill intent, sarcasm, or being overly critical. Taking a breath and thinking of how you come across can make all the difference.

Ask yourself, "Am I coming across in a way that will help me achieve my desired outcome?"

Professionalism

Imagine if when I went to my doctor for my panic attack, she had responded to me and said, "You came to see me because your itty-bitty heart was beating too fast? Give me a break. Stop being a punk and go deal with your problems like a man." That wouldn't be a very professional thing to say. Let's say someone on your team is presenting an idea for solving a customer problem and after they're done one of the executives says, "WTF did we just listen to? That was complete garbage and I don't know how you got this job." Again, not a professional thing to do.

Professionalism is what wraps around the Vulnerability Wheel and is about acting in a way that is either accepted or respected for the position you're in. As a leader, chances are you won't be in that exact same role forever; eventually you will move on and someone else will take your place. We all need to act or behave in a professional manner, which is all about how you get your job done.

The CEO of an investment firm told me: "Leading with vulnerability is a game changer, but of course it needs to be done in the context of the business environment that the leader is in. This doesn't mean turning your company into a big therapy session. Act in a way you would be proud of if tomorrow it showed up on the front page of every newspaper."

Ask yourself, "Am I exercising good judgment and acting in a way that is accepted or respected of my role?"

As a leader it's important to keep these things in mind, but there's a balance between preparation versus being scripted. If you sit down and map, plan, and rehearse everything, it won't come off as being authentic. In some situations, it can make more sense to sit and think through these as you saw in Chapter 22 with Jim Fitterling from Dow Chemical, who took a very methodical approach with how he came out, first with his board, then his leadership team, and then the company. In most scenarios a quick mental check will be all that you need to make sure that your vulnerability will achieve desired outcomes.

For example, let's say you're having a one-on-one conversation with someone on your team who is sharing that they are going through a tough time and you want to share that you are also struggling with something. You can walk through this wheel:

Intention:

> Question: Why do I want to share that I'm also struggling with someone on my team?
> Answer: It will create trust and connection.

Who:

> Question: Do I know whom I'm being vulnerable with and do I trust them?
> Answer: Yes, a new team member whom I trust has good intentions.

When:

> Question: Is now a good time to share something personal or should I ask this person to grab coffee later so we can talk in more detail?
> Answer: Now is great because we have time to talk.

Tone:

Question: How am I going to share what I want to say in a way that has the highest chance of achieving my purpose?

Answer: I can let my guard down, show emotion, and talk as if I'm speaking with a friend.

Professionalism:

Question: Am I exercising good judgment and acting in a way that is accepted or respected of my role?

Answer: Yes, I'm being thoughtful of the other person and of myself, am representing myself with good intentions, and am doing what anyone in my role should do.

If you go through the Vulnerable Leader Wheel and you find that your response to any of the questions is "I don't know" or "no," then you should stop and try to get clarity before moving ahead.

For example, if you're not sure how your tone will come across, you can get feedback from a trusted friend or even family member. If you don't think now is a great time to tackle an issue, then find a better one. You get the idea. The point is you should have clarity about all of the elements in the Vulnerable Leader Wheel to help make sure that when you are vulnerable you have the greatest chance of a positive outcome.

Deb Cupp is the president of Microsoft North America; she is responsible for 10,000 employees and oversees a $67 billion-dollar business. Here's what she had to say about this framework: "The vulnerability wheel is a very useful framework for leaders. The five elements are important to think through so that you can make sure your message resonates with those around you and is received in the right way. Leading with vulnerability can yield amazing results in terms of connection and performance. Clarity and intention are powerful factors that contribute to leading with vulnerability."

24

The Vulnerability Mountain

The eight attributes help you become the vulnerable leader, The Vulnerability Wheel helps make sure you harness that power in the right way, and the vulnerability mountain gives you a starting point and a path to follow. You don't need to have all of the attributes before you begin your journey; some you will develop as you climb the mountain, and the ones you start with will only get stronger and more powerful the higher you climb.

What we consider to be vulnerable varies from person to person, and not everyone is comfortable with the same level of vulnerability. To become a vulnerable leader, you need a starting point, or if you have already started, you need a path to follow. If prior to reading this book you haven't been willing to be vulnerable at work and tomorrow you show up sharing your deepest and darkest fears and failures, then it will create more confusion and chaos than it will have a positive impact.

Where do you start? I recommend you build your vulnerability mountain and then climb it (see Figure 24.1)!

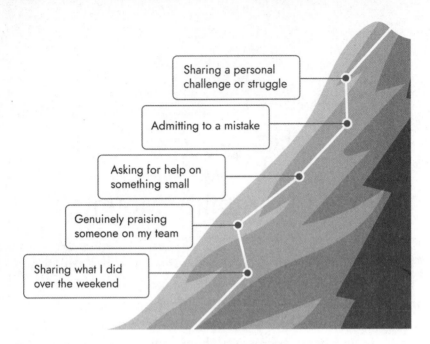

Figure 24.1   The vulnerability mountain

At the bottom of the mountain are the easier things you can do today. The higher up the mountain you go the more challenging the terrain becomes. For example, at the bottom of your mountain you might be asking for help or praising someone on your team, and higher up might be talking about a mistake you made or a personal challenge you are trying to overcome.

Each time you go higher on the mountain you reach a new vista where you can see the world and those around you with more clarity. Just like climbing a mountain, you will also have places where you set up camp and rest. This is also where you will find other people like you who are climbing that mountain with you and are on the same journey.

Sometimes as you climb the mountain you pick the wrong path and you have to go back down a bit in order to find a better path to keep climbing. Ascending this mountain becomes a part of your never-ending leadership journey, but the more you climb the more relationships you build and the deeper the connections become, the more clarity you get, the farther you can see, and the more beautiful the views become.

Deb Cupp, whom we met in Chapter 23, is one of the many of the vulnerability-embracing leaders featured in this book; she knows what it's like to climb the mountain:

> When conditions get tougher and the mountain gets steeper, it's all about putting one foot in front of the other, putting in the work, and focusing on what you can control. Being vulnerable can be challenging, but the ROI of being a vulnerable leader is incredibly high. When you're vulnerable, it makes people feel like they can better connect to you as a person, and it encourages them to show up as themselves at work. That creates a better environment for the team and for the business as a whole, especially when leading through change. Climbing the mountain is an ongoing journey filled with plenty of bumps and bruises along the way. It's a journey that every good leader signs up for when they agree to be responsible for others. It's hard work, but you, your team, and your organization deserve it.

Everyone's mountain is going to look different because we all experience vulnerability differently and what might appear at the bottom of one person's mountain might appear much higher up for someone else. To get a sense of what that range might look like for you, ask yourself two questions.

First, "What would I be willing to be vulnerable about right now?" This could be something that might sound a bit scary or uncomfortable but something you could handle. Then ask yourself the same question I asked the more than 100 CEOs I interviewed. "What makes you feel most vulnerable and why?" That will give you a good idea where you can start your vulnerability mountain and where you can climb to.

As a leader the most important thing for you to remember is that you have to start climbing first before you ask others to climb with you, but you should never climb alone. Although as a leader you take that first step, you should invite others on your team to join you on the journey.

Remember, if you already have people working for you or if you have power, authority, or influence over others, then they already feel vulnerable toward you. By being vulnerable with them, it levels the playing field.

I recently learned this lesson in a very heart-wrenching way. For several years I had a really big supporter of my work who was based in Europe. He signed up for all my courses, recommended my work to his network, and was a great ambassador and evangelist of my ideas and content. We never met in person but we exchanged countless emails and frequently spoke via virtual calls. We were even planning on hosting an in-person event one day and talked about how much fun it would be to get together. We exchanged some pleasantries here and there but most of our conversations were focused on business. My wife started a virtual community of customer experience professionals where they would have weekly calls, and at the very beginning there were a handful of people who joined, including him.

One day as I was scrolling through LinkedIn, I started to see some messages and comments that were very disturbing. A few people were writing RIP messages and saying that this person—my friend—had passed away. I thought it was some kind of a sick joke and I spent several hours that morning messaging everyone I could to find out what was going on. A few of his friends reached out to me and, sadly, the posts were true. He was gone.

One of his friends offered to speak with me on the phone and it was one of the hardest conversations I've had. She told me that he thought the world of me and my wife, that he really respected me and called me his friend, and that he was so excited about collaborating with me.

She then told me he was going through a lot of personal problems and challenges in his life but that he didn't want to be vulnerable with me because he thought I would think negatively of him and that I would think his personal problems would detract from some of the things we were trying to do together. She also told me that he didn't die from natural causes but that he committed suicide.

The last thing he posted on his LinkedIn page was some nice words about me and a webinar we did together. I was gutted. After I got off the phone I cried. I cried because I lost a friend and because I felt like a complete failure who let someone down in the worst possible way.

I spend a lot of time talking about leadership, connecting with others, putting people first, and being vulnerable. I failed to create a space where he could be vulnerable with me and share some of the things he was going through. Worse, I never made enough effort to ask or to be vulnerable with him so he felt safe to be vulnerable with me.

Had I known about any of his challenges, maybe I could have helped in some way or offered support. Knowing that he thought so highly of me yet didn't feel like he could be vulnerable with me felt like getting hit with a ton of bricks. Here I am writing a book about being leading with vulnerability and someone whom I have known for several years didn't feel like they could be vulnerable with me. He wasn't vulnerable with me because he didn't know I had my own problems and challenges that I was dealing with, just like he was, just like we all are. We all have problems, none of us are perfect, and we all need to be kind to one another and support each other.

This is an especially crucial lesson for leaders because it means you have to lead by example. To create a culture that encourages and accepts vulnerability and to create a team of vulnerable leaders, it has to start with you. You cannot encourage others to be vulnerable if you are not vulnerable yourself.

Richard Baldridge is the former CEO and current vice chairman of Viasat, a global telecommunications company with almost 7,000 employees. In the 1980s, he worked at a company called Joel Dynamics and he was always the most junior guy traveling around on private planes with the top executives and presidents of various company units. He worked 80 hours a week and was flying all over the place. Most of the time they didn't have a flight attendant on board, and because Richard was the most junior employee he'd be the one to pass out the food. On one of these trips he flew with the CEO of the company and it was time for breakfast so Richard got out of his seat ready to serve the others on the plane. The CEO looked at him and said, "No, Rick, you sit down. I got this."

He said, "This made an enormous impression on me. I thought that all these other leaders were wannabes, they acted superior and in charge, and they were willing to treat me differently than they treated each other. But not the CEO of the company. This profoundly changed how I interact with everybody to be more vulnerable and humble. Everybody looks perfect from a distance but when you get up close you realize that we are all human beings filled with mistakes, failures, vulnerabilities, insecurities, and frailties."

Climbing a mountain isn't easy. It is daunting, you will get hurt on your journey, and it takes time. The hardest part of the climb is base camp because it's overwhelming to imagine the trek to the top. The best time to start is now. I've been climbing the mountain for a few years, and it's tough.

Not everyone is willing to make the climb but you do it because the higher you go the more you transform yourself and everyone around you. You climb the mountain to become the vulnerable leader, a superhero with tremendous power and responsibility to create positive lasting change. When other people at base camp see you climb and succeed by being vulnerable then they will do the same and climb the mountain with you. I truly believe that if we can create more vulnerable leaders, our organizations and the world will be a better place.

Remember that a vulnerable leader is a leader who intentionally opens herself up to the potential of emotional harm while taking action (when possible) to create a positive outcome.

It's about bringing together two components—vulnerability, which is about connecting with people, and leadership, which is about being great at what you do. If you can do both of these things, then you will be able to lead through change and positively affect the lives of those around you.

I hope this book has inspired you to lead with vulnerability and has given you the data you need, the frameworks you can apply, and the stories you can use to support your efforts. Challenge your leadership stereotypes, identify what kind of superhero you are, focus on creating positive outcomes and avoid a fixed mindset, develop the eight attributes of vulnerable leaders, and then start climbing the vulnerability mountain. Today is the beginning of your journey to lead with vulnerability. Once you make that first step there is no going back. You will achieve more for yourself, you will create trust with your teams, and you will improve the performance of your organization.

I come from a family of survivors who always had to be resilient and strong. My dad always taught me to be tough and not vulnerable and that's how I lived most of my life. Being a strong leader is valuable, but leading with vulnerability is what enables you to connect with others and change the world.

I still have a long way to go and a lot to learn. We need more superheroes. I'll see you on the mountain.

Notes

Chapter 3

1. Hart, H. (2018, May 15). What a butterfly species' "lethal evolutionary trap" teaches about wildlife conservation. *Texas Standard*. https://www.texasstandard.org/stories/what-a-butterfly-species-lethal-evolutionary-trap-teaches-about-wildlife-conservation/
2. https://en.wikipedia.org/wiki/Evolutionary_mismatch#:~:text=The%20mismatch%20theory%20is%20when,the%20present%20create%20immediate%20results
3. Sheridan, M. B. (1993, September 29). The roughest, toughest bosses—Fortune crowns seven meanies. *The Seattle Times*. https://archive.seattletimes.com/archive/?date=19930929&slug=1723534
4. Wood Brooks, A. (2014). Get excited: Reappraising pre-performance anxiety as excitement. *Journal of Experimental Psychology*, *143*(3), 1144–1158. https://www.apa.org/pubs/journals/releases/xge-a0035325.pdf

Chapter 4

1. Ely, R. J., & Meyerson, D. (2008). Unmasking manly men. *Harvard Business Review* (July–August).

Chapter 10

1. Belle, D., Tartarilla, A. B., Wapman, M., et al. (2021). "I can't operate; that boy is my son!": Gender schemas and a classic riddle. *Sex Roles*, *85*, 161–171. https://doi.org/10.1007/s11199–020–01211–4
2. Leary, M. R., & Cox, C. B. (2008). Belongingness motivation: A mainspring of social action. In J. Y. Shah & W. L. Gardner (Eds.), *Handbook of motivation science* (pp. 27–40). Guilford Press.

3. Bordeaux, C., Grace, B., & Sabherwal, N. (2021, November 23). Elevating the workforce experience: The belonging relationship. *Deloitte*. https://www2.deloitte.com/us/en/blog/human-capital-blog/2021/what-is-belonging-in-the-workplace.html

4. Schwartz, J., Mallon, D., & Eaton, K. (2021, July 21). The worker-employer relationship disrupted: If we're not a family, what are we? *Deloitte*. https://www2.deloitte.com/us/en/insights/focus/human-capital-trends/2021/the-evolving-employer-employee-relationship.html

Chapter 14

1. Gymnastics History. (2021, November 17). 1968: Věra Čáslavská's beam score and the problems with judging. https://www.gymnastics-history.com/2021/11/1968-vera-caslavskas-beam-score-and-the-problems-with-judging/#more-1483

Chapter 15

1. Jiang, L., Kouchaki, M., Gino, F., et al. (2020, February 10). Fostering perceptions of authenticity via sensitive self-disclosure. Harvard Business School. https://hbswk.hbs.edu/item/fostering-perceptions-of-authenticity-via-sensitive-self-disclosure

2. Jiang, L. Kouchaki, M., & John, L. K. (2023, January 11). Research: Why leaders should be open about their flaws. *Harvard Business Review*. https://hbr.org/2023/01/research-why-leaders-should-be-open-about-their-flaws

Chapter 19

1. Coyle, D. (2018, February 20). How showing vulnerability helps build a stronger team. Ideas.TED.com. https://ideas.ted.com/how-showing-vulnerability-helps-build-a-stronger-team/

2. Smith, E. E. (2019, January 9). Your flaws are probably more attractive than you think they are. *The Atlantic*. https://www.theatlantic.com/health/archive/2019/01/beautiful-mess-vulnerability/579892/

3. Brooks, A. W., Gino, F., & Schweitzer, M. E. (2015). Smart people ask me for (my) advice: Seeking advice boosts perceptions of competence. *Management Science*, *61*(6), 1421–1435. http://dx.doi.org/10.1287/mnsc.2014.2054

4. Aronian, L. (2022). We're here to excite ourselves and the public. YouTube. https://www.youtube.com/watch?v=Gsbl9jhx_D0

Chapter 22

1. Mani, M. (2017, September 28). 12 short stories on self-realization and finding your true self. Outofstress.com. https://www.outofstress.com/self-realization-short-stories/#3_The_Teacup

2. Drucker, P. F. (2005, January). Managing oneself. *Harvard Business Review*. https://hbr.org/2005/01/managing-oneself; Brewer, K. L. (2022). Developing responsible, self-aware management: An authentic leadership development program case study. *The International Journal of Management Education*, *20*(3), 100697. https://doi.org/10.1016/j.ijme.2022.100697; Atwater, L. E., & Yammarino, F. J. (1992). Does self-other agreement on leadership perceptions moderate the validity of leadership and performance predictions? *Personnel Psychology*, *45*(1), 141–164. https://doi.org/10.1111/j.1744–6570.1992.tb00848.x; Tjan, A. K. (2012, July 19). How leaders become self-aware. *Harvard Business Review*. https://humanis.gr/wp-content/uploads/2022/02/How-Leaders-Become-Self-Aware.pdf; Zell, E., & Krizan, Z. (2014). Do people have insight into their abilities? A metasynthesis. *Perspectives on Psychological Science*, *9*(2), 111–125. https://doi.org/10.1177/1745691613518075; Dierdorff, E. C., & Rubin, R. S. (2015, March 13). Research: We're not very self-aware, especially at work. *Harvard Business Review*. https://www.aptusdiscovery.com/HBR_article2.pdf

Acknowledgments

As I've written in all of my previous books, each time one is published, it's accompanied by a major life event. When I wrote *The Collaborative Organization*, I was engaged; when I wrote *The Future of Work*, I was married; when I wrote *The Employee Experience Advantage*, I had become a dad to Naomi; with *The Future Leader*, my wife and I were expecting baby number two, Noah; and now with *Leading with Vulnerability*, Noah has officially been born, I'm a dad to two amazing kids, my family relocated from Northern to Southern California, and I had a panic attack!

My wife, Blake, is always my strongest advocate, supporter, and critic. She pushed me beyond the uncomfortable when writing this book and challenged me every step of the way to create something better than what I thought possible. She is an amazing wife, mother, friend, and partner in everything I do. My family, both here and in Australia, has been extremely supportive, especially when I was struggling with my panic attacks. Their support really helped me get through a tough time. Thank you and I love you.

Mom, thank you for always being there for me and modeling open communication and emotional support. Dad, thank you for always pushing me and challenging me to be the best that I can be. Neither of us are great with vulnerability but I'm hoping we can both embrace it more.

Stephanie and Rosey at DDI, thank you so much for believing in this work and for agreeing to be my research sponsors for this incredible project. Your help and analysis have really led to some fascinating insights and findings that will make an impact on leaders and organizations around the world.

I work with an incredible team who help me with everything from graphic design to podcast and video production to research and content management. Thank you, Allen, Briana, Charlie, Daryll, Ivon, Magdalena, Mhyla, Michelle, Mohan, Mubsher, Vlada, and Vlatko. I appreciate you all very much and am so grateful to work with you. Thank you to the team at John Wiley & Sons for helping get this book out.

To all of the CEOs, legal teams, and PR teams who helped make these interviews possible, thank you so very much for opening up, for sharing, and for being vulnerable with me. This book would not have been possible without you.

Last, I want to thank you for picking up a copy of this book and reading it. Thank you to my community of supporters who challenge me, share my content, and support my ideas and messages; you help make all of the work I do possible.

About the Author

Jacob is a professionally trained futurist, keynote speaker, and the international best-selling author of five books that focus on leadership, the future of work, and employee experience. His passion and mission are to create great leaders, engaged employees, and future-ready organizations. He is also the host of *Great Leadership with Jacob Morgan*, one of the most popular leadership podcasts. His work has been endorsed by the CEOs of Unilever, Cisco, Mastercard, Nestle, Best Buy, The Home Depot, Panera Brands, SAP, KPMG, T-Mobile, Audi, Kaiser Permanente, and many others. Jacob has also contributed to and been cited in publications such as *The Wall Street Journal*, NPR, CNN, the *MIT Sloan Management Review*, *USA Today*, *Forbes*, the BBC, and the *Harvard Business Review*. Jacob lives in Los Angeles, California, with his amazing wife, Blake, their two kids, Naomi and Noah, and their two Yorkie rescue dogs, Athena and Blinnie. You can learn more about Jacob and get in touch with him at TheFutureOrganization.com or via email at Jacob@thefutureorganization.com.

Index